DESIGN

An Owner's Manual for Learning, Living, and Leading with Purpose

Anthony J. Marchese, Ph.D.

WESTBOW
PRESS®
A DIVISION OF THOMAS NELSON
& ZONDERVAN

WestBow Press books may be ordered through booksellers or by contacting:

WestBow Press
A Division of Thomas Nelson & Zondervan
1663 Liberty Drive
Bloomington, IN 47403
www.westbowpress.com
1 (866) 928-1240

"Sweet Darkness" reproduced by permission from the author, David Whyte, *The House of Belonging* (Langley, WA: Many Rivers Press, 1997), 23.

"Please Hear What I'm Not Saying" reproduced by permission from the author, Charles C. Finn, *Please Hear What I'm not Saying: A Poem's Reach Around the World* (Bloomington, IN: Author House, 2011), 4-6; written in September 1966.

Cover image by Royce Stanley Dunn. Used by permission.

ISBN: 978-1-5127-7516-7 (sc)
ISBN: 978-1-5127-7517-4 (hc)
ISBN: 978-1-5127-7515-0 (e)

Library of Congress Control Number: 2017901809

Print information available on the last page.

WestBow Press rev. date: 2/23/2017

Dedication

This book is dedicated to my parents, Tony and Michele Marchese:

Mom, by encouraging me to wonder, you granted me an incredible gift.

Dad, you showed me it's never too late to live your dreams.

Sweet Darkness

When your eyes are tired
the world is tired also.

When your vision has gone
no part of the world can find you.

Time to go into the dark
where the night has eyes
to recognize its own.

There you can be sure
you are not beyond love.

The dark will be your womb
tonight.

The night will give you a horizon
further than you can see.

You must learn one thing:
the world was made to be free in.

Give up all the other worlds
except the one to which you belong.

Sometimes it takes darkness and the sweet
confinement of your aloneness
to learn

anything or anyone
that does not bring you alive
is too small for you.

—David Whyte

Contents

Foreword

"Design is the application of intent—the opposite of happenstance, and the antidote to accident." Robert Peters

"Design is the conscious effort to impose a meaningful order." Victor Papanek

With this book, Tony Marchese has hit a home run—not in the crowded "self-help" genre, but in the less-appreciated realm of "self-knowledge." He shows how shining a light on our true selves enables us to find hidden treasures, bring forth our best gifts, and make them part of our daily lives. Let me explain why I think Tony's simple, heartfelt approach to gaining self-knowledge is so important to individuals and to society.

I have been a teacher, consultant, board member, and community leader for more than fifty years. During that time, I have interacted with people of all ages, from all walks of life—children and youth, graduate students, pastors, business CEOs, staff members at nonprofit agencies, and community leaders. Often my role is to help these individuals develop strategies to improve the organizations and communities they serve. I've seen people make tremendous progress and do amazing things. The process is always faster and smoother when I'm working with leaders who are already aware of their strengths.

Many books extol the virtues of leaders getting to know themselves in order to be effective, and I think they are on the right track. Most of those books, however, don't offer a straightforward process for "plumbing the depths" and applying that new knowledge in practical ways. This book does. For so many people, this is the missing element needed to make a meaningful and lasting difference. In the pages that follow, Tony shares his own journey toward living a life true to his own design, and guides readers through a highly personal process they can use to do the same.

When Tony talks about "design," he doesn't mean a life design that someone else imposes on you, or one you impose on yourself. In his view, the collection of abilities, traits, and preferences that make you unique (Design with a capital "D") is already there, buried inside you. Your mission, like Dorothy's in *The Wizard of Oz*, is to find your way home—to yourself, and to the life you are perfectly designed to live.

If you're a leader (and everyone is, formally or informally, as a teacher, parent, pastor, coach, consultant, CEO, or in some other role), do yourself and those you lead a favor: Read this book, and go through the process Tony shares in the last chapter to discover your own Design. If you've had some leadership success, but find yourself falling short of truly making a difference, the self-knowledge you gain can help you bridge the gap.

Now is the time to discover your Design, so that you can use that knowledge to help others understand and reach their own potential. Imagine what might happen if we unlocked the best within us, and put it to work in our schools, churches, businesses, and communities. This is going to be exciting!

Douglas J. Walters, President
Transformation Specialists, LP

Acknowledgments

Writing a book about self-discovery is an act of transparency. When I started, the thought of sharing my thoughts and personal experiences on paper filled me with trepidation. Would readers find it interesting and helpful, as I hoped? Or would they consider it self-indulgent? As I recorded my stories of triumph and tragedy, however, a strange thing happened. These worries were replaced with feelings of gratitude and wonder as I recognized the enormous contributions others had made to my life, for better or worse.

The discoveries shared in this book would not have been possible without people whose words and actions affirmed my potential to climb even the highest mountain peaks to make a positive contribution to this world. A surprising discovery I made while writing was that people whose crippling words thrust me into the loneliest of valleys also played a significant role.

To both parties, I say "Thank you."

Why thank both parties? Because challenges as well as triumphs gave me the motivation and fortitude to explore the Big Questions about human purposefulness. *Design* is my humble attempt to synthesize twenty years' worth of musings—previously shared through college lectures, published journal articles, sermon notes, motivational talks, and creative writing—into a short, actionable framework for introspection, epiphany, and meaningful change. Should only one person find his or her life richer because of this work, I will consider my efforts immensely successful.

I would like to especially thank the following individuals for their exceptional contributions:

Carla McClure—I have long been an admirer of your ability to communicate the written word effectively. I am most grateful and humbled that you were willing to serve as my Editor in Chief.

Doug Walters, Travis Cooper, and Phillip McClure—Thank you for reading and rereading my manuscript. Your impressions and suggestions were carefully considered and are reflected throughout its pages.

Dr. Kimberly Hambrick—Thank you so much for your advocacy for this project. I hope it touches the lives of many.

Kimberly Cook—Your words of encouragement mean a great deal. You did a great job transcribing my lengthy interview.

Royce Stanley Dunn—Your painting, "Tree of Life, Pearls of Wisdom," perfectly illustrates the colorful tapestry of human potential, nurtured by a rich inner life.

Anthony J. Marchese, Ph.D.
November 15, 2016

Introduction

It was 3 a.m. when thirst woke me from a sound sleep and compelled me into the kitchen for a long drink of cool water. Too many slices of salty pizza for dinner, I guess. As I put down my empty glass, something on the kitchen table caught my eye: the owner's manual for my new cell phone. Still half asleep, I picked it up and thumbed through it. *Almost all products are sold with instructions,* I mused, *but most people don't read them unless they absolutely have to in order to make something work.*

This thought was quickly followed by another: *What if each person came with an owner's manual, based on his or her design features? What information would my manual contain? What would be different about my life if I lived it according to a set of instructions based on my individual design?*

I flipped to the table of contents and noticed that the instruction manual for my phone was divided into five sections—Overview, Distinguishing Features, Requirements for Optimal Functioning, Precautions, and Support. My semiconscious mind was connecting dots and pondering possibilities. *What if I had a personal owner's manual with these sections, filled with information customized to my "make and model," so to speak?*

These late-night/early morning thoughts were so strangely stimulating that I ruled out sleep and made myself a cup of coffee. If the section titles pertained to a person instead of a phone, what would they be like? I grabbed a notepad and jotted down ideas as they flowed into my mind:

1. Who I Am and Why I'm Here (Overview)
2. My Unique Attributes—The Things that Make Me, *Me* (Distinguishing Features)
3. What I Need to Be at My Best (Requirements for Optimal Functioning)
4. How I Can Prevent Harm to Myself or Others (Precautions)
5. Who I Can Turn To When I'm Not at My Best, or Need a Boost (Support)

Imagine having access to this kind of highly personalized information. Now, that would be a manual worth reading! Personally and professionally, it would affect the way I learn, the way I live, and the way I lead.

I glanced at the clock: It was 3:45 a.m., and I was fully awake. At the top of the page, I wrote "Book Idea." Under that, I wrote "Design: Developing Your Personal Owner's Manual."

Apparently, instead of sleeping, I was going to start writing a book.

A Little About Me

I consider myself a fortunate man. For more than twenty years, I've lived a life devoted to learning and leading.

From the time I was a child, I've had an insatiable hunger for knowledge. I fed this hunger by pursuing formal academic studies in a variety of disciplines, including theology, philosophy, law, organizational leadership, and positive psychology. During my doctoral studies, my dissertation committee allowed me to address key questions through an integrated or interdisciplinary lens of inquiry. This approach helped me create an inquisitive narrative — a carefully woven tapestry of diverse ideas and compelling research questions that, in turn, drove even more questions, and greater learning.

My professional life has proven to be equally diverse. I've worked in churches, nonprofit organizations, a host of universities, and international consulting firms. I've led projects and classes on a wide range of topics, including personal and organizational development. I've learned with and from people from all walks of life.

In these many contexts, I've been drawn to the phenomenon of leadership—but not as you may think of it. Plenty of books have been written about how best to direct small and large groups of people toward a desired outcome. I am grateful for these books of best practices. My interest in leadership, however, pertains to leading oneself toward a life of intentionality, of purpose. That's what this book is about.

Full disclosure: I'm a theist. I believe that every human who has ever lived possesses evidence of God's creative fingerprints. These "fingerprints," when examined closely, reveal much about how we are uniquely made. Our passions, proficiencies, preferences, and personality speak a great deal about ourselves that can help shape many of our significant choices. In my view, taking the time to discover, affirm, develop, and deploy these gifts is an authentic act of acknowledgment and worship. Nevertheless, belief in a divine creator is not a prerequisite for discovering your unique Design, or for benefitting from this book.

A Lot About You

This book is a beacon to anyone who has drifted far away from themselves. Maybe over time, as life happened, you've made concessions. Maybe you did so in order to survive, or because you were afraid. Regardless of the reason, today you might feel you've become "someone else" or are "playing the part" in a script you didn't write. Or you might feel caught up in circumstances beyond your control, disconnected from your past, present, or future. If you're reading these words right now, you've come to the right place, at the right time.

The pages that follow won't route you through a series of unfamiliar paths, but toward your true self. Rather than proposing strategies contrived by a stranger (me), this book offers a framework through which you can access and organize the wealth of information you already hold inside—information that can drastically impact the quality of your personal and professional life. You are invited to pause, ponder, and plan.

In no way is this book intended as an exhaustive guide to self-actualized living. Neither is it intended exclusively for people in professional leadership roles. The truth is, all of us are leaders of our own lives. This book was written with a firm conviction that humans are beautifully complex, and that living out of that complexity produces internal and external joy. A guiding assumption is this:

**Self-awareness is intimately connected
to positive leadership impact.**

This book will awaken in you an awareness that you are magnificently made. It will also challenge you to critically assess who you are, and where you are. Whether you are leading others or striving to lead yourself in this complex and often confusing world, the practice of becoming self-aware can feel risky, but it offers many rewards. Fred Rogers said it best: "Discovering the truth about ourselves is a lifetime's work, but it's worth the effort."

In junior high school, one of my English teachers' favorite phrases was "Life is not a dress rehearsal." While I've forgotten much of what she taught about participles and gerunds, this proclamation resides in me to this day. If we have only one shot at this life, are we choosing to be fully present in all that we do? Are we aware of the "design features" that are uniquely ours—our gifts, passions, personality, and proficiencies? Do we understand these features well enough to use them effectively in our day-to-day lives? Are we calling on this knowledge to ensure that we are maximally engaged in meaningful activities and interactions at school, at work, and elsewhere?

Pondering such questions, and uncovering who we are and how we belong to this world, is the way to determine what belongs inside our *Personal Owner's Manual*. I won't lie. It can be unnerving. At first, we might feel dismayed as we realize that much of our life's investment in school, work, or other endeavors seems far removed from what it should be, given our Design. If that happens to you, remember: No experience is meaningless. Each one has played a necessary role in bringing you to the place in which you now find yourself. Those experiences have prepared you to ask the right questions, and positioned you to discover answers.

So there is no need to wait until you "know enough" or "have experienced enough" to start asking questions that matter. *Now* is the ideal time to hit the Pause button on your normal routine, consider the rewards of an examined life, and begin an exciting journey toward a life truly worth living—one lived according to your Design.

How to Use This Book

The book is divided into four chapters. The first three chapters will inspire you to consider the way you learn, the way you live, and the way you lead. The last chapter will guide you through a process for developing your very own *Personal Owner's Manual*.

I suggest that you read the first three chapters before you start creating your *Personal Owner's Manual*. The stories and examples in these chapters will prompt you to think about your own experiences. If a passage sparks a personal memory, feel free to stop and examine it. Clues from your past can remind you of who you are and help you move toward your desired future. Knowing and understanding yourself will help you develop self-leadership.

Be patient. Self-leadership happens inside you, and it doesn't develop fully overnight. Have faith in the process. Devoting time to internal work will lead to external results.

Be strong. Developing self-leadership requires much of you. Throughout this book, you'll be asked to look back as you move ahead. This may be painful at times. You'll remember what it was like when your world seemed new, infinite, and ready to be conquered. You'll think back to an earlier time when your identity was emerging through your keen interests and talents. You'll relive and respond to words from others that diminished your self-worth, and to the words of those who made you feel invincible. You'll consider how formal education may have cultivated a transactional orientation toward learning that thwarted personal development, creativity, and investment in your work. You'll notice how your attitudes toward learning affect your professional work, and might make you feel disengaged. You might encounter memories that you haven't thought of in years. That's OK. Pause and examine them. Then keep going.

Be your true self. Chapter Four presents thoughtful questions that will help you imagine and articulate your *Personal Owner's Manual.* It will also help you integrate this knowledge into meaningful strategies to move from a state of mere existence to one of being fully alive. As you develop self-leadership, you will start feeling and acting more and more like your true, best self.

Let the discoveries begin.

Chapter One: Learning by Design

Two Kinds of Intelligence

There are two kinds of intelligence: one acquired,
as a child in school memorizes facts and concepts
from books and from what the teacher says,
collecting information from the traditional sciences
as well as from the new sciences.
With such intelligence you rise in the world.
You get ranked ahead or behind others
in regard to your competence in retaining
information. You stroll with this intelligence
in and out of fields of knowledge, getting always more
marks on your preserving tablets.
There is another kind of tablet, one
already completed and preserved inside you.
A spring over*flow*ing its springbox. A freshness
in the center of the chest. This other intelligence
does not turn yellow or stagnate. It's fluid,
and it doesn't move from outside to inside
through the conduits of plumbing-learning.
The second knowing is a fountainhead
from within you, moving out.
— Rumi

Recovering Wonder

One of my greatest joys in life is to spend time with others
engaged in the sacred exercise of self-discovery. Jointly exploring

1

one's personality, passions, proficiencies, and preferences can help illuminate the path that was always there, just difficult to discern. Days filled with excessive noise distract us from the attentiveness required to discover our identity and purpose in this life. Whether I am speaking with college freshmen or a room full of executives, the story is often the same. We have strayed far from our *birthright gifts*. We find ourselves at a place in our journey where the noise no longer keeps us fully distracted. We yearn for the peace that comes from knowing that our desires and capabilities are attuned to the needs of our world. When we are out of tune, we might feel hollow, or wooden, or depressed. We have lost our sense of wonder.

A while back, I wrote about this loss in my journal:

The Door

In the stillness of consciousness, there exists a place of infinite possibility. Colored by the creative pigment of imagination, it lies just beyond a secret passageway protected by a rugged door with a creaky handle discolored by accumulated dust. Behind the door is a pocket of time beyond the life-taking powers of routines, deadlines, and appointments—a state of being that defies every arrogant effort to diminish our magnificence and power through "reasonableness" and "maturity." This magical place allows us to fly at higher altitudes and faster speeds than even the fastest jets, and to warp ourselves through linear time.

As adults, when we think of that once-familiar place, it's usually through the lens of nostalgia, as we recall our childhood. Oh how often I've wished to return to that carefree life of innocence and, yes, ignorance! But I cannot. The realities of adulthood forced me to grow up. Yes, there are advantages to adulthood: I've evolved, and in various ways, I'm smarter and more successful than I was back then. Yet old home videos have the power to transport me to the Utopia of a past that now seems like a fantastic dream. That box of childhood treasures is still in my parents' attic, with a torn, stained cape inside, and that first blanket, which used to talk to me. What happened? How did life become so predictable and sterile?

Sadly, for many people, the brightly lit passageway to infinite possibility has become nearly impassable, blocked by the undergrowth and brush of worldly concerns. That magical place, streaming with vibrant colors and multidimensional worlds, now exists in a forbidden realm, posted with warnings: irresponsible, daydreaming, laziness.

Many who try to make their way through the tempestuous sea of seriousness and the briars of busyness to a place of timelessness won't get past that ancient door that opened for us so easily as children. For we have forgotten how to unlock it. Or maybe the posted warning scares us off before we even try. Besides, there is a report due tomorrow, and the cell phone is ringing. Year after year, our minds become more entangled with worldly growth, blocking our way. Unless we resist, it is almost certain that our vow of "this worldliness" will strangle the fresh air of creativity right out of our minds. We become casualties in our own society, still breathing even after we've died of self-inflicted wounds to the imagination. We've bought into the American dream, which says, "Produce, Work, and Produce More! The more you do, the more you are! Start early! It's time to grow up!"

Childhood is perhaps the most honest season of our lives. When we're young, we have yet to yield to the cacophony of voices competing for our attention. Parents, teachers, television, and connected culture present various compelling visions of our future selves, with promises of acceptance, approval, prestige, beauty, and wealth. We slowly yield our still-emerging dreams and gifts (not yet developed into talents) to acquiesce to the expectations of others. Part of us ("our real self") gradually backs away into the shadows. Eventually, we may find ourselves in middle age enjoying all the accoutrements of personal and professional success, yet strangely longing for something more gratifying.

Spiritual writer John O'Donohue (1997) explains, "Unless your heart is childlike and alive in a childlike way, then you are not able to wonder. One of the saddest things about the arrogance and power in modern culture is that it has killed the sense of wonder. So many people are walking around as mere functionaries, trapped in the metallic relentlessness of routines—precisely because they have killed the sense of wonder in their lives. They have lost a sensibility which can wonder. They have become so addicted to facts, to routine, to surfaces, and externalities that none of the deep darkness out of which the miracle of light emerges from within them seems to touch them or be close to them anymore. Wonder is one of the most special characteristics of the human person.... The imagination of God was able to create such diffuse and colorful and wild and beautiful diversity, precisely because the source and home of all wonder is in the divine imagination."

Where has the Wonder gone?

The Nothing

My absolute number one favorite movie as a child was *The Neverending Story*. I'm sure I've watched it at least fifty times. The movie tells the story of a boy named Bastian who, like me, escaped the treacherous world of adolescent awkwardness through reading books. An unleashed imagination allows us to run free through the extraordinary landscape of human creativity. This world of possibility and hope makes the lifestyles of adults seem like exercises in futility, as they constantly busy themselves with activities and therapies promising deliverance from the curse of predictability and boredom.

Bastian is introduced to an incredible new reading experience due to a heightened ability to stifle his awareness of his environment. As the sights and sounds of the room in which he reads slowly fade away, he sees, hears, and feels everything that the characters in the story see, hear, and feel.

Transported to the fictitious world of Fantasia, Bastian joins the young purple buffalo hunter Atreyu on a quest. An invisible force called *The Nothing* is quickly enveloping everything in its path, rendering all space void, threatening to obliterate this magical world. Atreyu and Bastian try to stop it.

As Bastian quietly follows Atreyu on his journey, he meets many of the inhabitants of this strange land, including gnomes, a Rock Biter, a Luck Dragon, and Gmork, the servant of *The Nothing*. As Atreyu nears the end of the quest, nearly losing his life a couple of times, he encounters Gmork, a large, talking, panther-like creature. Their startling conversation as Atreyu is confronted with the identity of *The Nothing* conveys a deeply meaningful message. Gmork explains that Fantasia is actually a place derived from human fantasy, containing the hopes and dreams of every person who has ever lived. The death of this magical world is a result of the dissolution of human hopes and dreams. *The Nothing* is a destructive emptiness that grows stronger day by day as Fantasia grows weaker. A loss of wonder, hope, and dreams renders human beings easily controllable, as they no longer have anything to live for.

When we are young, we are unaware of *The Nothing*. The terminal illness of evaporated wonder that adults suffer is usually unimportant to us. They have their world and we have ours. Though we are excited about one day becoming one of the "big people" and being able to enjoy a career as an astronaut or a fireman, and to even have children of our own, the possibility of our minds becoming old is an unexplored concept. As far as we know, the excitement of this life will always be a perpetual present. Life will always be one big adventure.

But *The Nothing* attacks his prey slowly and subtly. He works through the persuasive marketing strategies of television, the internet and magazines that encourage twelve-year-olds to be more conscious of their physical appearance and social image.

The Nothing even works through what many have lauded as exciting technological developments in children's toys. The lights, sounds, and motion leave young children in a quandary as they try to distinguish which is more real: their battery-operated toy car or their parents' Chevy in the driveway. Their senses are instantly stimulated by the toys themselves. The heavier demands of the outdated, obsolete toys of previous generations leave children wondering how their parents and grandparents ever had any fun with silent dolls and action figures. Often ignored is that fact that modern advances in electronic gadgetry stimulate the senses but retard the imagination.

The Nothing also works through popular television shows that portray tweens in heavily involved relationships with the opposite sex. In these shows, taking on the pressures of premature intimate relationships is depicted as normal. It is expected. The pure innocence of childhood is no longer desirable. Childhood becomes a disease to be cured by early exposure to *The Nothing*. Once the young have helplessly succumbed to the temptation to eat of the fruit that looks so delicious on the outside, they become drones at his command.

But the experience often leaves a bitter taste, as the pursuit of a highly romanticized self eventually leaves the victim regretful.

This regret signals that the skilled attacker has done a thorough job, as we become fearful of the future, haunted by the present, and nostalgic about the past. Time has a new meaning for us. We end up spending much of our lives looking back, reminiscing about how things used to be. In *The Sacred Journey*, theologian Frederick Buechner (1982) describes our perception of time before we experienced The Fall:

> What child, when snow is on the ground, stops to remember that not long ago the ground was snowless? It is by its content rather than its duration that a child knows time, by its quality rather than its quantity—happy times and sad times, the time the rabbit bit your finger, the time you had your first taste of bananas and cream, the time you were crying yourself to sleep when somebody came and lay down beside you in the dark for comfort. Childhood's time is Adam and Eve's time before they left the garden for good and from that time on divided everything into before and after. (pp. 9-10)

When we are young, we seldom look back. We usually look ahead, eagerly anticipating what new adventure awaits. Because of the fast-paced, consumptive society we live in, however, childhood arrives and departs in the blink of an eye. The unspoken dialog goes something like this:

Culture: It's time to put the toys away and start thinking about your future. What do you want to be?
Child: But I'm only twelve. I don't know!
Culture: Never mind. I'll tell you what to be.

Soon thereafter, we bury our childhood wonder and, with the last shovel of dirt, start anticipating the privileges of emerging adulthood. Driving our first car, proposing to our high school sweetheart, sending the kids off to college, considering what to do after retirement. Where has the time gone? The nagging pain in our neck could easily be attributed to the onset of old age, but perhaps its origin is of a more peculiar sort. Maybe it all started that sunny afternoon so many years ago when we boxed up our childhood toys and stashed them in the attic. From then on, time took on a new meaning and quality (fear of the future, avoidance of the now, nostalgia for the past).

So where does this leave us? Now that the ground over the grave of our childhood has settled and sprouted weeds, is it impossible to resurrect the child's sense of wonder? Now that we're empty and searching, are we doomed to continue as limp puppets in the hands of commercial industry, popular culture, and societal expectations? Is satisfying our internal restlessness simply a matter of finding whatever products or experiences promise the greatest immediate return? *The Nothing* wants you to say yes to these questions. *The Nothing* wants you to believe resistance is futile.

The Nothing is wrong! The way to resist *The Nothing* is to embrace wonder. It's not too late, and it's not as hard as you might think. But recovering wonder does require you to knock on its door, turn its creaky handle, and step across the threshold into a place of maybe's, options, and possibilities.

Leaving the safety and comfort of a predictable if boring existence to experience a wonder-full life might seem scary at first. But wonder is the prerequisite to learning, living, and leading by Design. And living by Design is the most effective way to battle *The Nothing,* which wants you to believe your brief terrestrial appearance is inconsequential and impotent. *The Nothing* knows it will be vanquished if you claim your power, take up your quest, and prepare yourself to contribute to this world as only you can do.

A good way to start your quest is to recall a time when wonder was an everyday experience. For most of us, that time was childhood—a time of "eternal now" when play was as essential as air. Below I share a story from my own childhood. As you read, I hope it will trigger memories of the people, places, sights, sounds, smells, tastes, events, and magical moments that fired your young imagination and made you feel fully alive in the present.

Always Make Time to Play

The clicking of the van's turn signal alerted me that our destination was near. As my mother turned onto the familiar gravel road, I saw a large, hand-painted sign prominently displayed for all to see: **Apples, Cider, Grapes: Last House**. A flush of satisfaction warmed my face. Grandpa and I painted that sign last week in anticipation of the year's apple and grape harvest. I was proud of our work and hoped that my grandparents' garage, now converted into a little country store, was quickly emptying its inventory. The tiny space was filled with bushels and peck baskets of Concord, Catawba, and Niagara grapes and Northern Spy and Wolf River apples, displayed on red-and-white checkered tablecloths. There were also shelves of fresh apple cider, free of additives and preservatives, meticulously made with a blend of apples.

As we pulled around to the side of the garage, a couple of winemakers were loading grapes into their cars, and Grandma was weighing a small box of grapes on the big white Toledo scale inside the garage as a customer opened her purse to pay. Like most visitors, the woman had probably tried a free sample, and

Grandma had likely relayed Grandpa's standard instructions to first-time samplers. "Eating a concord grape for the first time can be startling," Grandpa would often say. "Most people aren't used to eating grapes with seeds, especially varieties that are tart. When you eat a concord grape, you should firmly squeeze the grape into your mouth, making sure you get all the sweet juice. Don't chew it. Swallow it and then throw away the skin."

As my mom and I walked toward the front of the garage, the soothing sound of wind chimes was transmitted to all ends of the wooded front yard by an unseasonably warm fall breeze. A plump red squirrel carried a hickory nut in its mouth as it skittered past us and disappeared into a pile of leaves. When we entered the garage door, Grandma looked pleased. "We sold twenty bushel of grapes today and received an order for another ten," she said. "Grandpa is on his way up from the barn."

In the mid-1960s, my grandparents had purchased an 1800s farmhouse situated on twenty acres. Over time, it was restored to its former glory (and then some) as it became a working farm boasting a vineyard of six rows (300 feet each) of grapes, an apple orchard, peaches, raspberries, blackberries, soybeans, corn, a stocked pond, rabbits, chickens, and a barn with six horses. Attached to the garage was a woodshop, which supported a thriving antique restoration business. Twice a year, I would join my grandparents for the multiday journey to the Shipshewana Antique Auction in Indiana, where we'd sell refinished tables, chairs, glassware, and more. Retiring as a union carpenter just meant that Grandpa relocated his work almost entirely to the farm.

The side door opened, and a tall bearded man entered the garage, looking like he'd just stepped out of a Western. He wore a brown cowboy hat and boots, a red flannel shirt tucked into his jeans, and had a large belt buckle with a highly polished stone in its center. Grandpa. He smiled, glanced around the garage, and said, "Hi Tone. It looks like our sign did the trick. Are you ready to get to work? We've got a busy day ahead."

I said good-bye to Mom and Grandma, got a handful of grapes, and followed Grandpa toward the barn. Princess walked out of the stable and waited for us at the edge of the fence, snorting and stomping her hooves. She was either greeting us or demanding her share of my grapes. I approached her, scratched her mane, and extended my other hand with the grapes. Her tongue tickled my fingers, and the grapes disappeared in an instant. I wiped my hands on my jeans and ran to the back of the barn to catch up with Grandpa.

He was wrapping a heavy steel chain around the towing bar of the old Aliss-Chalmers tractor. That red tractor was nearly fifty years old, but it could do anything. Six years earlier, when I was only five, Grandpa and my older cousins used it to pull down an aging barn near the front of the property. That same chain had effortlessly brought the century-old structure to the ground. I smiled as I recalled what happened next. After the barn came down, Grandpa got off the tractor to admire the massive pile of wood. But he forgot to shift the tractor into park. As though driven by a ghost, the tractor bolted away from us and headed straight for the pond. Grandpa ran so fast toward the speeding tractor that he lost his cowboy hat. Luckily, he caught the tractor in time!

Now, as Grandpa chewed on a sesame-seeded breadstick, he grabbed a chainsaw and pulled himself onto the tractor's bouncy red seat. I grabbed a nearby green Thermos of cider and plastic cups, climbed onto the fender, and secured my footing. The tractor roared to life, and we were off!

Today we were cutting down an oak tree! We went past the big hill, the pond, and the vineyard toward the narrow grassy path between the freshly plowed field and the woods. Grandpa steered through an opening in the long pine tree barrier and stopped. I felt tiny as I stared up toward the top of the dead oak.

Grandpa positioned me a safe distance from the tree, then went to work with his chainsaw. A few minutes later, there was a loud crack, followed by a thump that shook the ground. The tree had fallen. Grandpa began cutting off its branches. My job was to drag them into a pile far out of the way. They would be burned later.

The whir of the chainsaw suddenly stopped as Grandpa switched on the choke and set it on the ground. He walked toward the tree stump that remained and said, "Tony, come over here. I want to show you something." He pointed down at the smooth surface of the stump. "Do you see all those rings? Each ring represents a year that the tree was alive. Count them." I quickly counted the clearly visible, reddish-orange lines etched into the stump, then counted again to be sure. "There are 85 rings," I said. He looked at me with his deep blue eyes and spoke in a reflective tone. "This tree is very old. Think about what this tree has seen in its 85 years—all of the history, all of the people it has met. Think about all the stories it could tell."

After that, Grandpa maneuvered the tractor to the heaviest end of the tree and asked me to uncoil the chain. Once that was done, he announced that it was time for a break. I found the Thermos and cups, and we sat on the enormous oak log. Grandpa poured the crisp apple cider, reached into his front shirt pocket, and brought out a bag of sunflower seeds. He looked at me.

"Tony, later on, we're going to work on that book of yours. We'll go into the woodshop and design the cover just the way you want it. We've worked hard today. We have to work if we want to eat. But remember, a man always has to make time to play."

I pondered his words. Almost every week, I worked with him at the farm. We'd start early in the morning but always finished by early afternoon. Our work would consist of cleaning out the barns, hoisting heavy rolls of netting across the grape rows, trimming the apple trees and grapes, cutting down trees, chopping wood, hauling and stacking wood, refinishing furniture, picking grapes and apples, or cutting the massive yard with a push mower. A few months earlier, he'd invited me to help him build ramps for people in the community who had handicaps. We also constructed decks for individuals from church. He taught me to log my hours so that I could be paid. There was always a right way and a lazy way to do something, and he taught me the difference. No matter how hard we worked or how difficult the day, however, we always made time for play.

Grandpa taught me how to make and shoot a bow, how to craft a wooden duck decoy (to be placed in the pond), how to run down a hill at an angle to avoid falling, how to load and fire a rifle (with accuracy!), how to build a multilevel fort, how to create and display a rock collection, how to navigate the woods without getting lost, and how to climb onto a horse and ride it. Grandma and Grandpa's house was a place unlike any other. Driving down that gravel road toward their house was like entering another world—one where I could explore, create, and thrive. The house at the end of the road was a place where I could be me.

That year, for my entry in the annual *Young Author's* competition, I had decided to take a nontraditional approach to the story and its presentation. It was a story of adventure and the unexplained. Because my grandparents' property was the setting for the book, it seemed natural for me to involve them in its production. The front and back covers were to be made of wood. Grandpa and I drew a picture of a pond and a tree, traced them onto a thin board, and used a jigsaw to make cutouts, which I sanded with great care. The pond was painted blue, the tree was painted brown and green, and the background and back cover were red. I used a heavy black marker to write on the front: "The Next Dimension: By Tony Marchese." The covers and the inside pages would later be bound with leather.

In lieu of pencil-drawn illustrations, I'd asked Grandma a week earlier to take photos for the book. She was an excellent photographer, and anytime family members were present, she was likely to have her beloved 35mm camera hanging from a strap around her neck. For the book, she spent a day in the woods with me. I would describe the scene I wanted, then act it out. She snapped pictures of me running down the hill, exploring the woods, simulating walking through a tree, taking a break to eat an apple, and falling into the water. Once the book covers were ready, Grandma was going to start typing my story and helping me arrange a layout with the photos.

Grandpa and I were in the final stages of affixing the two cutouts to the painted front cover with carpenter's glue when the dinner bell rang. Grandpa looked at me and said, "Let's go eat. I am hungry as a horse. Grandma made something good for us." We left the book covers on the deck of the table saw to dry, turned off the radio (which was playing 1970s country music), and headed toward the house. I walked ahead of Grandpa, pulled open the screen door, and looked at the large brass door knocker with a big "H" prominently displayed. Though Grandma was expecting us, I slammed the door knocker hard because I liked the way it sounded. "Come in," she called.

The smell of the wood-burning stove, baked apples, steaming roast beef, and green beans made my stomach growl with anticipation. At a small table in the corner sat her typewriter, a ruler, pencils, and a thick packet of pictures. All would be spread out on the big oak kitchen table after dinner for our work session.

Grandma was a multifaceted learner and educator. Like Grandpa, she was actively involved with 4-H as an instructor. While Grandpa taught gun safety, she led cooking and baking classes. She regularly spoke at area garden clubs about how to prune and propagate grapes and apples, and how to identify, care for, and dry flowers. They both volunteered countless hours on church committees, fundraisers, and planning for the county fair. An avid traveler, Grandma would take hundreds of pictures, convert them into slides, create a script, and conduct travelogue presentations to entertain family and friends. She was a perfectionist in all things. As we finished praying and started to eat, I knew one thing: By the end of the evening, the inside of my book was going to look great!

The Next Dimension

by Tony Marchese

Just outside of the city there is a short gravel road. That road leads to a special place I would like to tell you about. At the very end of the road is my grandparents' house. And it is there that my story begins.

One day something happened there that I'll never forget. I always did like to go walking in the quiet fields and woods, where all the sounds you can hear are the sounds of the wild animals, the birds, and the wind in the trees. It was on this special day that I went on my amazing adventure.

I asked my grandfather if I could go for a walk and he said it would be OK, but be sure to be back by supper-time. And so, I was on my way.

I passed the grassy hill, the pond, our favorite place to fish, across the open field to the giant oak tree. On I went to the creek, which I crossed. A few minutes later I reached the woods.

Soon I found a clearing and a big log where I sat down to eat the lunch that I had packed earlier.

Just as I finished eating, I heard a noise that sounded like frogs croaking. I looked around, trying to find where the noise was coming from. Down through the trees lay a small pool of water. It looked like a miniature lake. There, sitting near the end of the water was a huge, olive-green bullfrog. Reaching in, trying to catch him, I fell into the water.

Then, a strange thing happened. I couldn't pull myself out of the water. A very strong current was pulling me deeper. There was just no bottom. There was one thing, though, that really puzzled me. How could I be under water and still be able to breathe? After I was pulled in even deeper, the water was changing color. From light blue to red—red to yellow. What was happening to me?

Then there was total blackness; no water, no trees, not anything. Where in the world was I? I must be out of this world! Just then a bright light shone in my eyes. I was frightened and yet excited with the anticipation of what would happen next.

Then everything looked normal again, but the temperature had dropped suddenly. Then I heard a rustling noise. Quickly looking around, I saw a squirrel walking toward a tree. Never had I seen such a slow-moving animal

before. It jumped toward the tree to climb it, but it went right through the tree!
It seemed to be like a ghost passing through a wall.

I looked toward the sky and saw a bird flying. At least, I thought it was
flying. It saw a mouse and swooped down to catch it. When it touched the
mouse, it went right through it and disappeared. It was a very slow bird.
Everything in this world seemed to be in slow motion. When the wind blew,
the trees moved ever so slowly.

Then I had an idea. I walked over to a tree and reached over to touch it,
but fell right through it. This was impossible, I told myself over and over
again. But I knew it was real. Everything seemed to be moving at a very
slow pace, and nothing seemed to have solid matter. The strange pool was a
door to another dimension. Then, all of a sudden, I began feeling drowsy and
was getting a headache. I wasn't sure why I felt this way so quickly. I tried
walking, hoping it would make me feel better. But there seemed to be some
strange force holding me back as if it didn't want me to go anywhere.

I began to wonder what my grandparents would say if I didn't get back soon.
So I looked at my watch to see what time it was. I had been in this strange
world only ten minutes. It seemed like I had been there a long, long time.

I looked around me. Everything seemed to be in a sort of haze. After that
everything just faded away and that was the last thing I remembered until
I found myself sitting by the strange pool of water where it all had started.
Then, far off in the distance, I heard a noise that sounded like a police siren.
Immediately, I started running toward the house.

I had never run so fast in all my life as I did then. After about five minutes
I reached the house. There were two policemen taking notes as they talked to
my mother and father. They had several tracking dogs with them. Everyone
ran up to me, asking me several questions. They all wanted to know where I
had been. I tried explaining to them what had happened to me. But they said

I must have fallen asleep and had a dream about everything. They also told me that I had been missing for three days. Three days!!! I had only been gone on my walk for forty-five minutes. I showed them my watch to prove it but they said that it must have been broken. But I KNEW THE TRUTH! I had been somewhere no one else had ever been: I had been to THE NEXT DIMENSION!

And the next time I hear an old bullfrog croak, I'll just smile, and remember, and just walk away.

THE END

The oak table that once belonged to my grandparents is now in my own dining room. As I sit at that familiar table, turning the pages of that book conceived by my younger self and created with their help, I notice the expression on my face in the photo illustrations. Though I was "acting" as Grandma snapped those pictures, in many ways, I was living my *own* story—one filled with as much adventure as novels, movies, television shows, and video games.

My personal story, however, was not without *directors*. Grandma and Grandpa, neither of them college educated, thoughtfully considered how to make every one of my visits with them a wonderful balance of hard work and magical play. Enchanted themselves with the world around them, they orchestrated diverse activities to prepare me for the vocation of life. I learned many lessons from them, but perhaps the most unforgettable was to *always make time for play.*

We often walked through the fields, especially after they had been plowed, in search of Native American artifacts. We'd find arrowheads, flints, and even axe heads. Grandpa would explain what each tool was for, and how it was used. He said he'd been told that his property was once the site of a Native American settlement. The elderly man from whom he'd bought the old farm described rolling hills that had been excavated in the early 20th century. We were both convinced that there had to be inconceivable treasure still hiding in the earth. I dug many holes during that time. I'd find bones, fossils, coins, and unidentifiable objects that fed my imagination. Fatigued, I would later fall asleep in a bed of soft needles under the pine meadow near the barn. I would dream of the ancient village and the battles that had been fought on the ground beneath where I lay. Once, I dreamed that I was camping in a small tent near the pond. In the dream, I was abruptly awakened by the shaking of the ground below me. A small, gray flying saucer had landed very close to my tent!

As a kid, hiking to the Big Oak Tree with Grandma, Grandpa, and my sisters and brother was always a very big deal. It was one of the most massive trees any of us had ever seen in Michigan. All of us would circle the tree, spread our arms as wide as we could, and interlock our hands to gauge the immensity of its trunk. Rarely did we bring enough people! I always looked up at all the squirrel nests concealed within the sprawling branches and wondered how many generations of families had made the Big Oak Tree their home over the two to three hundred years of its existence. Grandpa would tell us stories of what the terrain may have looked like when the acorn sprouted to life in the soil so many years ago.

Grandpa often let me rummage through the faded cardboard boxes in the outbuildings behind the barn. In them, I would discover yellowed newspapers, old books, magazines, and other "artifacts" from an era foreign to me. How fascinating it was to read news stories and advertisements from so long ago! People looked and spoke so differently! I'd bring a handful of items back to the house, and Grandma and Grandpa would talk with me about my treasures. They even allowed me to keep some of them.

When I was eight years old, Grandpa taught me how to read a carpenter's ruler and how to use a level. After my lesson, we walked out to the edge of his property to examine the place where I hoped we could build my first fort. We built every inch of it together. By the end of the weekend, a grand edifice had been constructed, with multiple levels and rooms. I even designed a contraption to allow running water to flow throughout the structure. I spent many nights there in the years that followed.

When I was twelve, I purchased my first raft with money I had earned working on the farm. Grandpa had spoken at length with me about how to survive in the woods. It was time to put my new knowledge to the test. I blew up my two-man raft and loaded it onto the trailer that Grandpa pulled with his garden tractor. It was nearly impossible for me to contain my excitement. We lifted the raft onto the creek's edge, and I stepped inside and sat down. Grandpa handed me my oar and my backpack. He gave the raft a big push, and I was gone. I didn't know where I would ultimately end up that day. I did know that it was possible that I could end up in Lake Erie. This would not be a good thing. The risk of my adventure coupled with Grandpa's trust in my abilities and judgement added much thrill to the experience. My backpack contained all that I would need. I had a pocket knife, compass, ham sandwich, apple, bottle of water, and walkie talkie. Grandma was monitoring the other radio back at the house. I will never forget all that I saw that day as I explored the unknown. I recall talking excitedly with them about my expedition over dinner later that evening. I'd make several more trips down Sandy Creek, often alone, but sometimes with friends. Each time, an adventure was guaranteed.

I think of those long-ago experiences as I close the cover of *The Next Dimension*. Next to the table where I sit is the matching oak buffet that once sat in my grandparents' dining room. When I open it, it still smells like their home. If only it could trap all of Grandpa's stories that were told in that room, the way it has retained the smell of their house.

The Nothing never successfully attacked Grandma and Grandpa. Even at an advanced age, they both remained active doing the things that brought them joy. Grandpa used to say that he wanted to die with his boots on.

When I visited his home shortly after his unexpected death, I was amazed to find so many wood carving projects that were in process. His work area was covered with hand-drawn patterns and all types of saws, chisels, and knives. There was not a speck of dust to be found on any of them. A load of recently chopped wood was neatly stacked next to the wood-burning stove. Canning supplies were readied on the porcelain table that Grandma always used. A book of Native American folklore lay open on the small table next to his recliner.

"Always make time to play." That was one of the valuable lessons I learned from Grandpa. My grandparents weren't professional educators, but they were amazing teachers.

Schooling: Cultivating or Constricting *Design*?

Today, education is a big business. Billions of dollars are invested annually to support efforts to improve student achievement and catapult the United States toward the top of international student performance benchmarks. Legislators, lobbyists, bureaucrats, and consultants serve as convincing advocates for new standards and strategies supported by research, statistics, and compelling promises.

No level of funding or research-laden reform, however, can consistently cultivate the proper climate for learning. More than any other factor within the education system, a highly effective teacher is paramount to student success. A skilled educator doesn't merely relay content, but generates within students a sense of curiosity and wonder—an insatiable yearning to take notice, ask questions, and find answers. A master teacher sees students not as blank slates to hijack in order to replicate the teacher's worldview. Instead, master teachers awaken students not only to the world around them but also to their unique gifts, and to their potential to learn and develop according to their own Design.

Excellent educators understand that learning is a sacred, highly individualized process that can either awaken a vocation or calling, or suffocate the joy out of its pursuit. They reject the one-size-fits-all approach to teaching and learning. That approach might seem efficient at first glance, but it ignores the grandeur of human diversity. The danger is that students will leave educational factories adequate in much but exceptional in very little. The world suffers immense loss every time a young person enters the workforce unaware of what makes him or her "tick" and how to tap into those unique attributes. When learning is attached only to job attainment, we are essentially denying our humanity to become little more than horses trained to pull a cart.

A proper education invokes wonder, inspires self-exploration, stimulates personal and professional development, and encourages civic contribution. It provides new ideas and experiences, but also meets learners where they are. Some are hands-on learners; they may watch intently but impatiently as their instructor demonstrates a task, as they are eager to do it themselves. Others learn by reading; they enjoy the mystical conversation between themselves and the author as they assimilate the knowledge and wisdom that's in the text. Both types of learners require exposure to new information, as well as opportunities to integrate that information into meaningful, personalized categories of understanding.

Learning not only provides new knowledge. It changes us. The movie *Dead Poet's Society* provides an example of a teacher who understands the power of education to awaken students to their potential. The teacher, Mr. Keating (played by Robin Williams), urges the students at an elite all-male prep school to resist the allure of cognitive conformity, embrace their unique attributes, and create a life according to their Design. To get his point across, he holds class in the school courtyard and invites each student to discover his own way of walking down an old brick path. Some students eagerly embrace the opportunity, while others hold back, unsure of themselves or of how others might react. For the risk-averse few, the potential for personal freedom is outweighed by the comforting predictability afforded them by a life of privilege. Mr. Keating urges them on: "Carpe diem! Seize the day. Make your lives extraordinary!" But they mistake the joy on the faces of their risk-taking classmates as foolishness rather than freedom. They wrongly think learning is an act of compliance rather than an opportunity to find their own way. They believe they are destined to jump through predetermined hoops to one day succeed their fathers in a legal, medical, or business profession that is their destiny. These false beliefs prevent them from even asking whether another path, or another way of walking it, might better suit them.

Design

Like most people, I was fortunate to learn from a couple of exceptionally gifted teachers, a few in elementary school and in high school. However, my lifelong commitment to personal and professional growth and my unquenchable curiosity is due, in large part, to yet another educator—someone who never formally studied teaching and learning and was not a professional teacher. In fact, she didn't take her first college class until she was in her 50s. However, she was an exemplar of personalized learning before it was invented and marketed to the masses as a best practice: my mother.

A Different Kind of Saturday Morning

The aroma of cinnamon-sprinkled French toast lingered in the house as I stood transfixed by the rhythmic whirr of the white sewing machine. It was Saturday morning, and my Mom, sister, and I had just returned from a young boy's most dreaded place—the fabric store! My sister, Heather, was now watching cartoons in the adjoining room, but not even the happy song of the Smurfs could pull me away from the bobbing of the threaded needle as it stitched the dark fabric beneath Mom's fingers. Today, she wasn't making a dress for Heather or an item to sell at the annual craft show. This time, she was making something for me.

It was no secret to my observant mother that I had an extremely active imagination. I spent hours every day reading science fiction and fantasy. Sometimes I used household items to contrive "inventions" in my room. A few Saturdays earlier, I had written a letter to NASA, then secretly acted out a space adventure in the living room with alien action figures and starships that roared to life at my command.

Starting today, however, a spaceship would no longer be necessary for travel to distant galaxies. My mom was making me a cape! In fact, she was making one for my beloved Winnie-the-Poo bear as well! Soon my bear and I would be soaring to the very top of the old walnut tree and inviting Rocky, my Boxer, to join us on an adventure in my secret hiding spot at the end of the alley.

Plato said, "Philosophy begins in wonder." So does learning. Education that's rooted in wonder captures a young person's attention, and urges the novice beyond the boundaries of current understandings. The best teachers personalize learning by inviting students to draw upon their natural gifts as they pursue new knowledge. That's exactly what Mom did for me.

My mother identified three of my *birthright gifts*. Like a skilled metallurgist, she handled each gift in a delicate but determined way to produce something of value—in my case, skills and interests that would last a lifetime. Whenever she saw a potential gift in me, whether it was emergent or uninhibited, she guided me toward experiences that would distill, clarify, and refine those gifts. She crafted an experiential curriculum grounded in wonder and used her time, talents, and treasure to provide it. We read and wrote stories together, and she provided countless trips to the county library for story hour, taught at-home cooking classes, and stayed up late at night to help with science fair projects.

Years later, I still have that cape. Just last night, I opened the heavy lid to my wooden trunk and pulled it out. I moved my fingers across the precise stitching and smiled. Only a couple of months earlier, during a conversation with my mother, she had said, "Tony, I would have made a good teacher." Instantly I pictured in my mind the long string of experiences she had provided throughout my childhood, and the proud look on her face as she watched me walk across the stage at my doctoral commencement ceremony. Without hesitation, I said, "You *are* a teacher!" Teaching is one of her *birthright gifts*. Like Mr. Keating in *Dead Poet's Society*, she helped me discover my own way of walking through the courtyard.

Postsecondary Learning

For more than twenty years, I've worked in education. I've witnessed firsthand how it can breathe life into people, especially those who've felt disenfranchised due to a lack of opportunities and financial resources. Some see postsecondary education as the key to breaking the cycle of poverty and opening up career options that their parents never had. Taking the steps necessary to land a career that provides intellectual stimulation, flexibility, and other rewards is a worthwhile endeavor—though the necessary academic preparation requires a substantial investment of time, effort, and resources. Why, then, do so many young people approach their education as they would the roulette table at a casino? Shouldn't choosing a career involve more than watching the wheel spin and hoping for the best? Is college nothing more than a series of trials and errors?

I've worked with numerous students who chose a career track based on little more than a fleeting interest or the hope of a big paycheck. A few weeks after they enter college, their poor performance in the prerequisite courses demands action. Classes are dropped, and the academic major is changed in hopes of a better match. This approach to finding the right academic program/career can be likened to paying at the gas pump for a car wash, then entering random numbers into the numeric keypad at the entry to the carwash bay, hoping to gain entry. Until the proper code is input, the light remains red and the door to the carwash bay stays closed. The light never seems to turn green, despite numerous visits to the keypad, and access to a promising future is denied.

Is there a better approach, one that ensures greater odds of finding the right career match? What can students do to reduce the likelihood of multiple changes in academic major, or entering a profession that leaves them dissatisfied? Here's a thought: What if college and career decisions were determined, in part, on a customized *Personal Owner's Manual?* How much happier students and parents alike would be if the planning process were driven with knowledge and intentionality rather than trial and error.

The collegiate environment provides a range of experiences that teach us about ourselves. We learn about our acumen for balancing multiple responsibilities like attending class, studying, living and working with others, choosing what clubs or organization to participate in, and making decisions about how to spend our "extra" time. These experiences help shape our choices as we move forward in life. Often, however, too much value is placed on learning from our mistakes in college, such as choosing the wrong major or spending too much time in an alcohol-induced stupor. Although everyone makes less-than-optimal choices in college, not all choices need to fall into the "wasteful" category. Yes, a year spent completing prerequisites for a mismatched academic major does produce new knowledge, but that year could be more productive and satisfying if we got it right the first time. The best way to make that happen is to make sure our choices are guided by self-knowledge—the kind found in our *Personal Owner's Manual.* Unfortunately, this manual can't be purchased in the campus bookstore. Equipping ourselves with a *Personal Owner's Manual* requires that we do the following:

- Identify our distinguishing characteristics (personality, passions, proficiencies) and *birthright gifts.*
- Consider our requirements for optimal functioning. (What do I need in order to be "at my best"?)

- Understand precautions for making sure we cause no harm to ourselves or others.
- Enlist a tangible system of support that can provide encouragement, insight, and strategies to help us focus and move forward.
- Contemplate and articulate our vocation or calling.

"In our society many people have worked extremely hard to pursue careers that pay well rather than fit their talents and interests. Such careers are straitjackets that in the long run stifle and dehumanize us. Disciplines and constraints, then, liberate us only when they fit with the reality of our nature and capacities. A fish, because it absorbs oxygen from water rather than air, is only free if it is restricted and limited to water. If we put it out on the grass, its freedom to move and even live is not enhanced, but destroyed. The fish dies if we do not honor the reality of its nature." Timothy Keller

Most colleges and universities require the successful completion of prerequisite courses before a student can matriculate into an academic discipline. Chief among these required courses is the infamous College 101, referred to within more progressive institutions as the First Year Experience. This credited course is designed to help acclimate students to college life and establish a foundation for positive performance in classes. As part of the course, students often tour the campus and learn where the library is located, where to go for health services, how to stay safe on campus, and how to report various kinds of harassment. They also learn important time management skills. Students may be provided with a day planner or smartphone application to encourage and reward effective task management, such as scheduling regular study time or workout sessions in the fitness center. These activities certainly support positive performance during the first year of college.

Nearly all first-year programs, however, focus on behaviors rather than individuals. This could result in students becoming adept at getting to the library but unable to connect what they read to their desired future. Or they might excel at creating a schedule but fail to follow it when difficulties arise and they don't know how to cope or how to get support. Such experiences can induce a feeling of detachment. This can put them at risk for failure because detachment impedes drive.

For most people, college is incredibly demanding, filled with emotional highs and lows, and replete with experiences that stretch their capacities. College can challenge people in new ways, helping them discover they're far more capable than they thought. It also presents unfamiliar situations and circumstances, and requires students to interact with a wide range of people and to negotiate personal relationships. Those who enter college with a clear sense of purpose and identity are better prepared to succeed in this complex and confusing landscape.

For anyone reading this who is currently preparing for college, here are some words of wisdom: Knowing who you are and how you are made makes it less likely that you will make choices that take you far from your true self and place you in danger. It also makes it more likely that you will choose a vocation or "calling" that honors your Design.

The process of discerning your Design may be supported by others, but must be confirmed by yourself. Only you know which activities ignite within you a sense of wonder reminiscent of childhood. Only you can sense when a task pays you back in full (plus gratuity) by connecting you to something far bigger than yourself. Pursuing a college education becomes a sacred act as you avail yourself of books, conversations, lectures, and internships that honor the "reality of [y]our nature" as Keller describes it.

A sense of identity and purpose will help you move beyond a merely transactional relationship with school or work, wherein you exchange effort for good grades or good pay. You will become attentive for clues to your *birthright gifts,* and college will become a sacred journey that prepares you for much more than just a job. Working through college within this framework will likely result in fewer dropped courses, better grades, and the immense satisfaction that comes from not just completing courses but discovering and nurturing your calling.

A Lifetime of Wonderful Learning

The Nothing works on everyone, regardless of age, position, or level of prosperity. Its goal is to render us free of joy, purpose, and power, to render life as merely transactional. When that happens, the world around us gradually loses its luster as we find ourselves feeling hollow and inconsequential. As we grow into adulthood, is it possible to fight *The Nothing?* Can we retain the awe of childhood while balancing the overwhelming demands of grown-up life? Is a lifetime devoted to learning possible? Or, in our chase after the American Dream, have we truly lost ourselves?

For those of us beyond the years of formal schooling, wonder need not fade from existence. A 1983 remake of an episode of a classic television series illustrates this point. In a segment of *Twilight Zone: The Movie* called "Kick the Can," a charismatic visitor named Mr. Bloom (played by Scatman Crothers) arrives at Sunnyvale Rest Home. There he invites residents to envision aging not as an end but an opportunity to continue doing things that bring joy. He polls them to find out what they enjoyed most about childhood. All excitedly share their most beloved memories of childhood play—except Mr. Conroy, a sour man who reminds the group that old people need their rest. Mr. Bloom counters, "The day we stop playing is the day we start getting old...start watching the clock, waiting for the days to hurry up and end... counting the years." He invites the group to a midnight game of Kick the Can, his favorite, reminding them that, as children, "We always had something to look forward to, another dawn, another day, another summer...another game of kick the can! So, who's playing?"

The Sunnyvale residents pledge to join Mr. Bloom late that night. They decide they will break the rules together, with the exception of Mr. Conroy, the rest home supervisor. At the specified hour, the elderly men and women gather in the yard and begin playing. Immediately, their voices and bodies are transformed into those of children. They climb, dance, sing, wield swords, and play on the swing set. One of them notices the still-elderly Mr. Bloom and asks why he doesn't join the group. Mr. Bloom responds, "I found out a long, long time ago, I wanted to be my own true age and try and keep a young mind. Your wish has come true; you're children again. You've got your whole life before you."

After Mr. Bloom's speech, the others voice reservations about remaining children. They discuss losing loved ones, the impossibility of meeting their spouses again, and maybe even worse, going back to school! Mr. Bloom smiles and says, "Well, you can always go inside and go back to bed. Maybe if you old folks had a little of that magic still left in you, you'd wake up back in your old nice bodies but with fresh, young minds—fresh young minds." The children begin repeating the phrase "fresh young minds."

The next morning, with young minds but once again elderly in body, the residents happily plan an outdoor picnic. A few watch Mr. Conroy, the resistor who didn't want to be awakened for the midnight game, as he concentrates on his own game of kick the can. Mr. Bloom, who's preparing to leave Sunnyvale, looks directly into the camera, smiles, and reassures the audience, "He'll get it. He'll get it." Moments later, we see Mr. Bloom arriving at a new rest home, ready to go to work.

Revealing a sobering realization while observing a group of young men and women participating in a televised cheerleading competition, David Whyte (2008) says,

> Here are all these astonishing young… men and women, (with) this incredible snappy, sharp ability to create all of these different dance figures and forms. It was youth incarnate. In the middle of it, I felt myself almost ready to weep and I asked myself what it was. I realized that in ten years time or twenty years time, or however long it took- but just a matter of time- all of those youthful faces would have their own signature of grief in them. They would have their own slowness and their inability to actually move with the same kind of alacrity of vitality or sense of arrival and that youth, in a sense is fated to grow older in the world. It is fated to come to understand it's imperfections. I think one of the great triumphs of human existence and one of the tasks of adulthood is actually to grow younger again- to find that youthfulness at each stage of our existence. There is a radical edge that's available to us no matter whether we're twenty, thirty, forty, fifty, or sixty. It just looks different at each stage.

Humans are endowed with an unrivaled capacity to learn. Our sense of wonder keeps it alive—and keeps *The Nothing* at bay. Understanding our unique Design enhances our ability to learn at any age, to reach our potential, and to contribute to society. Parents and teachers must resist "quick fixes" and cookie-cutter approaches to education for children and youth, as the consequences may be dire and long lasting. As adults, let's do our part to ensure that wonder remains alive and well at all stages of life, as its void makes living by Design an impossibility.

Notes

*Record memories, insights, and epiphanies here
so that you can refer to them later.*

Notes

Notes

Chapter Two: Living by Design

"The way to find your calling is to look at the way you were created. Your gifts have not emerged by accident." Timothy Keller

"The kind of work God usually calls you to is the kind of work (a) that you need most to do and (b) that the world most needs to have done.... The place God calls you to is the place where your deep gladness and the world's deep hunger meet." Frederick Buechner

"Every child is an artist. The problem is how to remain an artist once he grows up." Pablo Picasso

Living by Design

To say we live in contentious times is an understatement. Our cell phones, tablets, and televisions work tirelessly to keep us up-to-date on the scandal of the day. Wars, rumors of wars, racial discord, a volatile economy, impropriety within the electorate, the threat of foreign and domestic terrorism—the list has no end. Social media feeds our narcissistic tendencies by elevating everyone to the role of social and political commentator. Our compulsion to "vent" online, and to immediately agree or disagree with others' opinions, can short-circuit opportunities for reflection and dialog, make us feel frustrated, and even destroy relationships. Threats of severing decades-long friendships by deleting or blocking others run rampant within this virtual universe.

The barrage of negative notifications seems inescapable. Even the lunch hour offers no reprieve: Many professionals eat with a fork in one hand and a phone in the other. During the 2016 presidential election cycle, medical experts warned the public to restrict exposure to the media, as mental and physical health can be severely compromised by our response to vitriolic exchanges between candidates and parties.

An unexpected encounter during a recent business trip to Atlanta served as a poignant reminder that it doesn't have to be this way. Even in the midst of turmoil, there are mysterious forces at work that can quell our unrest. Individuals unlock those forces when they answer the call to live by Design.

Kameel: A Man from Nazareth

It's no secret that I appreciate fine food. My culinary passion was cultivated at my grandparents' kitchen table, where the family gathered each Sunday afternoon for spaghetti. There, my paternal grandfather taught me how fresh basil and grated Romano cheese added to its flavor. As soon I had my plate just right, our eating contest would begin. At age twelve, I finally beat him!

My passion for food continues to this day. As soon as I learn of an imminent trip to a new place, I scour online reviews to determine where I'll enjoy my meals. In anticipation of the conference in Atlanta, I was pleased to learn that the #1-rated restaurant in the city was within a few hundred feet of my hotel. The fact that it was Mediterranean made it even more exciting. The website for *Aviva by Kameel* promised "the friendliest, most helpful service and the freshest, best-tasting sandwiches, salads, and platters." It went on to say, "We want our guests to integrate Aviva into their daily healthy lifestyles through our fast service, welcoming atmosphere and, of course, delicious food."

I visited Aviva by Kameel for lunch the day after I checked into my hotel. It was located in the food court of a shopping center, with a long line of people outside, so it was easy to spot. My anticipation built. If so many people were willing to wait, it must be worth it!

Through the restaurant's glass enclosure, I could see that the place was immaculate. Its colorful walls displayed pictures of delectable dishes. The line moved quickly. Near the entrance, a large sign boasted a fantastic menu. The day's special was salmon and sea bass kabobs. My mouth watered.

Artfully displayed newspaper stories told about the restaurant, including pictures of its owner, Kameel Srouji, an emigrant from Nazareth. Aviva, which means "cleansing spring" in Hebrew, was named after his sister, who worked in the restaurant, as did Kameel's son. That day, the restaurant was celebrating its four-year anniversary at that location.

Suddenly a man in a white chef's uniform was standing in front of me, smiling. It was Kameel! "Welcome to Aviva," he said. "I am so glad you are here today. Please enjoy a bowl of seafood soup while you wait." A bit stunned by his friendliness, I was momentarily at a loss for words. Kameel continued, "This is your first time at Aviva. Thank you for sharing our fourth anniversary with us. I love you."

I realized this was not going to be a typical lunch experience. Who says "I love you" to a stranger? What, precisely, does he mean? Why did I sense such authenticity, right away? I watched as Kameel greeted patron after patron. Many received a hug. I heard him say "I love you" several times. People of all ages, ethnicities, and faiths (as evidenced by their clothing) were smiling after their brief interactions with Kameel.

Soon, I reached the counter and placed an order for kababs. Unfortunately, the demand for kababs had exceeded the day's supply. Suddenly, someone peeked out from the kitchen, waved at me, and said, "Please come back here. I have something to show you." It was Kameel. I stepped out of the line, and he took me to a prep area. "Here, try this. It is our other special of the day— crab-stuffed avocado. I think you will love it. It is orgasmic." He handed me a small plate with a generous portion. It was one of the best things I had ever tasted. Kameel called to his colleagues, "Please give him extra. He has waited for a while."

I took my food to a table and looked around the room. Employees wandered through the dining room with trays of fresh melon and tiramisu, which they offered to guests free of charge while expressing gratitude for their visit. On the wall in front of me, a large screen presented information about the Mediterranean diet and its health benefits, with the message "Eating well is a prescription both for the body as well as for the soul." Kameel went from table to table, thanking everyone for visiting, ending each conversation with a handshake or a hug and "God Bless You." Few customers were texting or talking on their phones. Instead they were speaking with one another, or with Kameel and his staff, or just thoughtfully enjoying their food. The room was filled with a serenity I've encountered nowhere else, not even church.

Aviva by Kameel is the #1 restaurant in Atlanta because it is an experience, not just a place with flavorful food. It offers patrons a temporary refuge from conflict and negativity. Why scan social media or news sites on your smartphone when you can engage with a man and his staff who may care more for you than you do yourself? Here was a place where people of all nationalities and creeds could enjoy the simple yet elusive elements of happiness: Love, Hospitality, Gratitude, Health, and Blessing Others.

I left the restaurant that afternoon beyond satisfied, yet hungry to know more about this man from Nazareth. As a student of organizational leadership, I've encountered a variety of individuals who lead in diverse ways. However, I couldn't think of any who functioned with such simple confidence and joy, and exerted such effortless influence.

The power to influence others is essential to effectiveness, according to leading authorities on organizational leadership. And there was no doubt that my lunch experience had affected me in a positive way. That morning, as I watched one negative news story after another, I had felt frustrated over the divisiveness within our country and abroad. After lunch at Aviva by Kameel, I felt empowered to do my part, to be a better member of the human race, to focus on what unites us rather than what separates us. Kameel was leading his staff and patrons toward a better life.

Throughout the afternoon, I kept thinking of questions that I wanted to ask Kameel. What had inspired him to create such an unusual dining experience for his customers? To what did he attribute his sense of mission? What did he mean when he told his customers he loved them? That evening, I decided to call the restaurant, hoping Kameel would be willing to talk with me. Though they had officially closed an hour earlier, his son answered the phone. A minute or so later, I was talking to Kameel. Although he had no doubt seen hundreds of customers that day, he immediately said, "I remember you well. I invited you into my kitchen."

I told him I'd had the best lunch experience of my life at his restaurant and explained that, as a student of organizational behavior, I very much wanted to learn more about his story. Kameel graciously said yes, and we decided to meet in my hotel lobby the next morning.

At 8:30 a.m., Kameel arrived and greeted me warmly. He carried two boxes of baklava. "The first box is for us to share as we talk," he explained. "The second is for you to take home with you." I took a bite of the baklava and smiled. Kameel said, "Most people use lots of butter when they make baklava. I use no butter. Instead, I use some of the finest olive oil that can be purchased. It is the best baklava you will ever eat. What do you think?"

My first thought was "This was going to be a great interview!"

Kameel described the process of emigrating to the United States many years ago with a passion for improving the lives of others through healthy eating. Obstacles that many would deem insurmountable only served to increase his sense of urgency in pursuing his dream. He believed it was important *not* to discount his dream because he ascribed it to someone larger than himself. Additionally, he believed that the place and time in which he found himself was aligned with a Divine imperative to live according to his Design. Kameel was concerned about the typical American diet and the debilitating health issues that accompany a lifestyle sprinkled with artificial flavorings, contaminated meats, preservatives, pesticides, and harmful fats. A long journey full of soaring mountaintops and desolate valleys had ultimately brought him to his current place—a place in which he sees evidence daily that by acknowledging his dreams, his giftedness, and his passion for health, he is in fact serving God.

Kameel and I talked for more than ninety minutes.

Named by area farmers as "Mr. American Produce," Kameel described his unwavering commitment to buy products organically grown in the United States. Though competitors often charge more in their restaurants for genetically modified products, Kameel believes it is his calling to feed his patrons "from God to mouth." This means that human attempts to improve an already wonderful piece of fruit or a fish will inevitably produce an inferior, likely harmful product.

Kameel is skeptical of much of the commercial food industry, as attempts to increase volume, inhibit spoilage, and reduce costs often come at a great price. Rampant obesity, cancers, diabetes, and other maladies are attributed to an uneducated or uninspired consumer base who, in the name of cost savings or busyness, chooses to offer little resistance to those grocery stores and restaurants offering harmful products.

Kameel described patron after patron who had experienced the significant health benefits of eating his organic products. Some patrons ate at his restaurant multiple times per week. Several experienced remarkable weight loss and overall wellness. Kameel explained, "My sister, Aviva, said 'God wanted you to come to America to make a difference with food, to change lives.' God brought me to America to spread the word of the Old Testament. Give them the best (food) because God loves the best. I am fascinated with Abraham, who took the biggest sheep God provided to him. It could have been another animal, but it was a sheep, clean and beautiful. Jesus became the lamb of God. There is a relationship to me. I tell my customers who come in here, I am going to give you from God to your mouth."

"I live in America. America protects me. I want to pay back American farmers. People are not well-educated about food and are in a hurry. Many would rather have a second home in Florida. I tell them to take care of their body because that is what God gave us. I tell my employees, every single customer who walks in that door is my boss and your boss. Without them we are not paying our bills. We are not getting paid. A priest recently wrote me a note that touched my heart and even gave me goosebumps. It said, 'God brought you here for a reason and you're showing it to your customers. That is the true Jesus in you.' I am going to continue in my path every single day. I want to get better every single day and I want to make sure my consumers are getting better every day."

Without a doubt, Kameel Srouji believes that he is living by Design. He views this life as a gift given with one string attached: To make others happier by offering food and education to make them healthier. Kameel lives his life with extreme intentionality. Awareness of his destiny buoys him during times of difficulty and uncertainty. The missional clarity through which Kameel views and leads his life is a force to be reckoned with. Hundreds of patrons darken his door on a daily basis, weakened and distracted by a myriad of stressors. With just a few words, a hug, and a heavenly meal, Kameel inspires a seismic shift in perspective.

What about that love comment that surprised me so? When I asked Kameel why he told customers he loved them, he responded, "I love you for not only coming in to eat my food but for supporting me. You allow me to help make lives better. What could be better than this? You're giving me life to keep going, to breathe, to spend my energy making the best food there is. In my mind and heart is a desire to give the best, so of course I'm going to love you."

Kameel then described an important lesson he hoped to teach his customers.

"I tell my customers, 'Guys, we need to love one another.' When you turn around at the church, you shake your neighbor's hand, right? What do you tell them?"

"Peace, peace be with you."

"I tell my customers the same thing. When you pass the falafel plate while you are waiting to order in the line, tell others that you love them. Because what's happening around the world is all about money and power. It is so sad. People have lost the feeling that God has brought us here for a reason. We're killing each other. I tell them to tell others that you love them because we need love."

Kameel's words inspire me similarly to those of Henri Nouwen, who wrote, "In a world so torn apart by rivalry, anger, and hatred, we have the privileged vocation to be living signs of a love that can bridge all divisions and heal all wounds." (p. 199).

The rest of this chapter explores how, like Kameel, we can become more sensitive to our giftedness, and cultivate it in order to make a profound and positive impact on our world.

Entelechies: The Creative Fingerprints of God

entelechy *noun* \en-'te-lə-kē\

1. the actualization of form-giving cause as contrasted with potential existence

2. a hypothetical agency not demonstrable by scientific methods that in some vitalist doctrines is considered an inherent regulating and directing force in the development and functioning of an organism

For thousands of years, theologians have sought to harmonize the ideas of ancient philosophers and the concepts in holy scripture. Though the Ancients did not possess the gift of special revelation, they discovered many important truths through a curious and critical examination of the external world. A concept discussed in detail nearly twenty-five hundred years ago by Aristotle was the very nature of reality. In a philosophical departure from Plato (his esteemed teacher), Aristotle emphasized not the externality of truth, but rather its immanence. In other words, he peered inward instead of looking outside and above.

Aristotle proclaimed that all living things contain hidden forces or drives ("entelechies") that, when properly nurtured, can move them beyond their potential toward a state of maturity or actualization. He illustrated his point with an example from nature: A seed that is planted in nutrient-rich soil and watered can transform into a magnificent tree.

Aristotle's seed metaphor can be applied to people. Within every human being is an impartation (seed) of unique attributes. With the proper care, the potentialities within metamorphose into tangible gifts. The development and deployment of these gifts allows the person to function naturally, thus executing his or her special mission. Recognizing our Design (and going one step further by crafting an accompanying *Personal Owner's Manual*) is a powerful way to ensure that entelechies mature and become manifest in meaningful ways.

In *The Widening Stream,* which is a tremendous work for those who aspire to be artists of any sort, David Ulrich (2002) further describes the concept of vital information that is embedded within us. He writes,

> In *The Soul's Code: In Search of Character and Calling,* James Hillman proposes what he calls the "acorn theory," that every individual has within themselves the seed of a unique calling, a daimon which accompanies the soul and is the "carrier of your destiny." He believes that every person is born with this inner image of completeness, much like an acorn, which later manifests as a mature oak by following a vague, yet persistent inner call. But our own inward calling only stays vague and unformed until we work to uncover the meaning found in these subtle intimations from within that mark our destiny and reveal our true selves. We have within us an inner measure, capable of separating truth from falsehood. How can the acorn know that it will become an oak tree? It cannot; yet deeply imprinted in its genetic code is that potentiality—and no other. We must remain true to ourselves; we have no other choice. Yet we need to listen and to bring a rigorous sense of discrimination to our inner impulses. The voice of our true nature is unmistakable, though not immediately apparent. We must learn to distinguish this essential call from the many voices of our personality that clamor for attention. We cannot predict its sound, but we can know something of its quality. It has a different resonance, a different ring than all the other inward songs. Our true nature lies within us, waiting to be discovered, or more to the point uncovered from the many years of conditioning that served to create a tough and inert outer crust over it. (p. 19)

Birthright Gifts

Thousands of years after Aristotle's introduction of embedded Design, educator and author Parker Palmer (2000) contemporized the concept of entelechies. In his stirring book, _Let Your Life Speak_, Palmer urges his readers to view themselves not merely as being shaped by circumstances or choices, but to look beneath the veil at what he calls "birthright gifts." His premise is that every human being is wonderfully and uniquely made. Though individuals and events may influence the trajectory of our lives, imprinted within us are deeply personal gifts that (when nurtured) reveal our best, most authentic selves.

Our giftedness should be handled with great care, as it is bestowed upon us by our Creator to help point us toward areas where we can do the greatest good. The most meaningful gift we can offer the world is that of giftedness fully affirmed and revealed. Palmer (2000) writes,

> We arrive in this world with _birthright gifts_. Then we spend the first half of our life abandoning them or letting others disabuse us of them. As young people we are surrounded by expectations that may have little to do with who we really are, expectations held by people not trying to discern our selfhood but to fit us into slots.... From the beginning, our lives lay down clues to selfhood and vocation, though the clues may be hard to decode. But trying to interpret them is profoundly worthwhile— especially when we are in our twenties or thirties or forties, feeling profoundly lost, having wandered, or been dragged, far away from our _birthright gifts_. (pp. 12, 15)

David Ulrich (2002) echoes Palmer's call to examine our gifts. He writes,

It is important to remember that we all have our place of genius, where we have something to offer that can grow only from ourselves. We strive to discover the seeds of our true individuality. It is often subtle, a whisper from within that needs time, nurturing, and a degree of challenge for its inward potential to emerge. Faint as it may be, we listen for its distinctive, clear rhythm amidst the confusing cacophony of our illusions, stray desires, and wishful thinking. We search for what is genuinely our own and we work to uncover our latent talents and skills. (p. 11)

Consider yourself invited to visit or create a quiet space, free of distractions and demands, where you can receive the invaluable gift of becoming reacquainted with your true self. You are beckoned to look at yourself anew, to recover the wonder you felt years ago when you felt, saw, heard, and tasted for the very first time. Intentional openness to discoveries about yourself is the way to rediscover your *birthright gifts*. Openness and self-reflection will likely ignite both revelation and responsibility as you think of ways you are uniquely made, and consider how you can meaningfully relate to the world around you. A story about my father demonstrates the power of *birthright gifts* to bring joy to ourselves and others.

A Special Reunion: Dad

Borgetto, Sicily—a cool breeze dampens the unforgiving Mediterranean mid-morning sun in this quaint coastal village. It's a Sunday in June, and men, women, and children in their finest suits and dresses emerge from their gray stone homes and walk the crowded streets toward the sound of the church bell, which beacons from the city center. Rich tomato sauce simmers on countless stoves, and the smell permeates the air. As hundreds of residents pack into St. Anthony's, anticipation of savoring a post-Mass meal is exceeded only by an urgency to be within earshot of *The Violinist* who is visiting the church this morning. Word has spread that Anthony Marchese, an American violinist, has come home.

Anthony is my father. His grandparents were born in this lush mountainous region but were part of a mass exodus to the United States a century ago. Like others, they left to pursue a dream of full-time work, bountiful mealtimes, and patch-free clothing. Now we, their descendants, have returned to this place for a visit.

In many ways, Borgetto hasn't changed much since my great-grandparents' departure long ago. Poor economic conditions continue to plague the region. Throughout the week, men of all ages gather outside businesses to enjoy steaming coffee and share stories of better times. Women, like their mothers before them, hone their craft within the kitchen, perfecting the art of doing much with very little. Young people aspire to improve their quality of life while affirming the sobering reality that a future consisting of a college education followed by a good-paying job may take them far away from their beloved families.

Today, however, the villagers' typical concerns seem to melt away as they enter St. Anthony's Church. Immediately upon entering the historic edifice, one is greeted with the sweet smell of incense and a vivid panoply of Biblical events captured forever within the thick, stained glass windows. A massive oil painting depicting Mary (the Mother of God) seizes the attention of all who enter this sacred place. How surreal for my father to look around at icons and art displayed just as they were when his grandparents made their weekly trek up the hill to worship with other members of their community.

Soft organ music plays as villagers seek a place to call their own—either tightly seated on a wooden pew or standing at the back of the sanctuary. The priest greets each of us warmly and motions for my parents and me to follow him into an antechamber, where he prays for and blesses each of us. His quick Sicilian is challenging to follow as he prays, but words such as "family," "love," "gift," "music," and "blessing" are stored in my psyche and imbued upon our spirits. (Later, we would all agree that while we didn't understand everything he said, the moment he laid his hands upon us was electrifying.)

My mother, visibly moved by the kindness of the priest, follows me out of the room to find a place to sit. The priest directs my father to the elevated platform where he sits in a place of honor next to our cousins, Andrea and Teresa Marchese. The music reaches a crescendo. The mass is about to begin.

My father closes his eyes briefly—likely trying to discern whether the strangely familiar sights, sounds, and smells of his surroundings are real, or part of a magnificent dream. Less than ten years earlier, at the age of fifty, a brain tumor, a series of strokes, and a heart condition had brought the blur of his 60+ hour workweeks to a jarring stillness. Operating on a brain tumor such as his was not without serious risks and later complications. Untreated, the slow-growing but debilitating tumor would be terminal. He'd opted for the surgery.

Afterward, thankful to be alive, my father quickly learned that nearly all of his faculties were impaired at some level. He suffered a loss of equilibrium, some deafness, diminished sensation of taste, and compromised eyesight. But he was alive, and he recognized that his life was at a crossroads. Returning to his job at General Motors was not an option. The only diploma he held was a GED, but his hard work had paid off over time. He had moved from the assembly line to a strategic role within the quality control department of the corporation. But times were tough for the company, as it was enduring bankruptcy proceedings, and current employees and retirees faced significant changes to their projected earnings. For countless families, the future looked increasingly bleak.

For many people, growing older is characterized by a series of sacrifices. We put away our toys, contain our youthful aspirations, enter into the daily grind of a demanding job, and do whatever is required to ensure that our children have all that they need and at least a little of what they want. My father knew this quite well.

But there was one kind of "play" he'd put away years earlier that his illness prompted him to resume. Unbeknownst to many of his friends and former coworkers, my father had been an accomplished musician as a young boy and teenager. During those formative years, locking himself in his bedroom to play his violin was a comforting reprieve from the physical and verbal abuse heaped on him by his (now deceased) father during alcohol-induced stupors. The deep tonality of the violin, coupled with the life-giving words of his mentor, Don Smith, affirmed my father's worth as a musician and most importantly, as a person.

He continued to play the violin for his own enjoyment for many years. Eventually, however, the demands of providing for a family of eight contributed to his decision to put away his violin. Unfortunately, only his older children shared memories of Dad playing *The Lone Ranger* theme song as we rode in sync with the music on our spring-driven rocking horses.

After his invasive brain surgery, however, the grueling hours, days, and months of recovery and rehabilitation provided him something of incalculable worth—a pause in the expected direction of his life. In his weakened state, he became overwhelmed with *wonder* as he pondered his existence and in particular, a certain *birthright gift*: music.

One day during his long recovery, he'd simply gotten up from his chair during a spaghetti dinner with the family and gone to his bedroom in search of his old violin. He found it in the closet in its smooth black leather case, which he dusted off and opened. The dense red velvet interior was even softer than he remembered as he lifted the violin, a rare gift from his father, from its case. How long had it been? Twenty years? He tucked the violin under his chin and took up the bow. The first few notes were awkward and strained. It was like becoming reacquainted with an old friend. Much had happened in the years since their last encounter. But like all meaningful relationships, within a few minutes, the conversation took on a life of its own. It became effortless.

Now, thousands of miles from his home in the United States, in the church where his ancestors once worshipped, he walks to the center of the stage, violin in hand. He is indeed awake. In fact, he is more alive and alert than ever.

The music begins. Dad opens with "Lord of the Dance," followed by "Ave Maria," and ends with "Amazing Grace."

The deafening applause and cheers following his performance affirm what he already knows. Though he did not enter the woods like Thoreau, he did, after his difficult journey, find himself arriving at a similar conclusion: "I went to the woods because I wished to live deliberately, to front only the essential facts of life, and see if I could not learn what it had to teach, and not, when I came to die, discover that I had not lived." (p. 90). After his performance, saying good-bye to the Marchese's of Borgetto and all his new friends would be hard, but twenty violin students were waiting for their teacher to come home.

###

Birthright gifts reveal the depth and breadth of human diversity. While we all share in common the presence of Design, the way our gifts manifest themselves is as unique to each of us as our DNA. Like discovering our place of origin, knowledge of our gifts serves as a stabilizing force as our identity and calling become clearer. Acknowledging and developing our gifts helps reveal our place on the brilliant tapestry of human experience.

Birthright gifts often reveal themselves very early in life. Like entelechies, they require nurturing and development over time. Both negative and positive experiences can create conditions that contribute to their development (e.g., difficult times that drove my father to the safety of his bedroom when he was a boy, and the encouragement of his mentor).

In the previous chapter, I discussed my mother's gift of observation during my childhood. She watched attentively for clues that might provide insight into my Design. My *Personal Owner's Manual* was being outlined, and I didn't even realize it! Often, external acknowledgment of our entelechies or *birthright gifts* pushes us toward their cultivation. Like a tiny seed eager to grow, they need the right conditions (soil, water, and sunlight) for germination. Recognition of our Design is often a gradual process shaped by impressions, experiences, conversations, and experimentation.

Discovering and Developing My Design

The tables that follow describe three of my *birthright gifts*: Preservation, Invention, and Illumination. Each table shows how one of these gifts initially manifested itself through various clues, how my parents responded to these clues, and how the gift developed and continues to present itself. Hopefully, reading these examples will spark ideas about your own gifts.

GIFT #1: Preservation—Preserving the Past to Maximize the Present

Clues	Parents' Response	Development and Presentation
— Interested in all things from the past — Fascinated by the rings of trees — Loved going to antique auctions — Collected old books — Enjoyed looking at old pictures and watching old family movies — Asked adults a lot of questions	— Gave me a cassette recorder and microphone for my ninth birthday. I used it to "capture" moments in time. I understood the temporality of existence, and the difference between past, present, and future. I wanted to be able to relive an experience by preserving it exactly how it was, so I recorded conversations during Sunday afternoon spaghetti dinners. — Encouraged my interest in photography and videography — Let me help grandfather restore antique furniture	— Journaling — Shared hundreds of recordings (30+ years old) with family for Christmas; own many of my family's heirlooms — Became a collector of antiquities — Traveled to numerous historical sites around the world

GIFT #2: Invention: Pursuing Creative Possibilities

Clues	Parents' Response	Development and Presentation
— Spent hours in my upstairs bedroom assembling items to perform a function, such as a talking robot — Enjoyed rewriting popular storylines from cartoons or envisioning new, better scenarios with my cartoon-inspired toys — Crafted day-long rafting adventures down the creek	— Encouraged participation in science fairs and in the Young Authors Contest and Conference — Helped me gather materials to create wood-burned plaques to sell at craft shows and garage sales — Allowed me to attend television production classes at a public access station — Enrolled me in piano lessons — Cheered for me when I started a DJ business at age 14, with financial support from my grandparents	— Writing and publishing — Hosted multiple educational television programs — Motivational speaking/ developing leaders — Coach individuals to discover and deploy their Design

GIFT #3: Illumination: Pushing the Mind Toward its Potential

Clues	Parents' Response	Development and Presentation
— Incessant questions: *Why? How?* — Fascinated by the boundlessness of outer space — Entranced by television programs and movies that pushed the limits of what was natural or normal, including *Star Trek*, *The Twilight Zone*, *The Neverending Story*, *Flight of the Navigator*, *Close Encounters of the Third Kind*, *E.T.*, *D.A.R.Y.L.*, *Mysterious Island*, *Superman* and lots of cartoons: *Voltron*, *ThunderCats*, *The Smurfs*, *Gummi Bears*, *Super Friends* — Restlessness: a compulsion to explore my world	— Purchased a book of questions and answers called *Tell Me Why* — Encouraged testing and participation in Talented and Gifted Program — Encouraged me to participate in competitive book reading programs (visited garage sales for books) — Gave me shortwave and CB radio for my birthdays — Showed me the community education schedule and encouraged participation — Supported my involvement in the local church youth group — Bought me a telescope for my birthday — Took me to NASA	— Lifetime learner: formal education resulted in degrees and certifications; also did lots of reading and mental calisthenics — College teaching: requires immersion in ideas — Facilitating presentations at national and international conferences — World travel — Finding mentors and interesting people who challenge my thinking and present possibilities

Dreamstealers

In all of my travels, public presentations, and classes taught, I have never encountered a person unfamiliar with the scars inflicted by a Dreamstealer. In his unconventional work *Dangerous Wonder*, Michael Yaconelli (1998) introduces Dreamstealers as people who, through their words and actions, deflate our greatest desires, rendering us pained, empty, and sometimes lost. Such individuals emerge within our lives in different forms, at various times, and are driven by a variety of intentions.

A Dreamstealer can manifest as a loving parent who, because of his or her own aversion to risk or lack of experience in a particular area, diminishes the value of his or her child's interests. Often, the last thing such parents would wish to do is to hurt their own; however, that's what happens when they steal the dreams of a loved one, perhaps in the name of being "realistic" or "responsible." Parents' handling of a child's destiny is a delicate matter.

Other Dreamstealers are far more sinister. They intentionally kill, steal, and destroy the dreams of others. Often they feel threatened by the world-changing potential they see in someone else, so they attack that person in a way that inflicts long-term damage: They target *birthright gifts*.

Regardless of a Dreamstealer's motivation or intent, many of their targets never recover from the Dreamstealer's attack. Often, their victims abandon their gifts, since they are now a source of immense pain and shame. The entire world suffers when the smoldering gift is extinguished. The impact of the loss of a nurtured gift is hard to quantify, but is nothing less than a tragedy.

For me, the most harmful attack of a Dreamstealer came during my senior year of high school. Like many students, I had chosen extracurricular or "nonessential" activities over academics. I had taken classes like radio production lab, music theory, speech, newspaper, and piano. Though I did well in those courses, my "academic" classes such as math and science suffered a bit. I knew that I had the potential to work harder and earn higher grades than C's, but I was content. I was actually having the time of my life.

One afternoon, while in class, a student worker delivered a note instructing me to report to my guidance counselor for a meeting later that day. I assumed it was the same "exit interview" the rest of my peers were required to complete before graduating. Although I knew my 2.7 GPA would not get me into Harvard, I was excited to let my counselor know I had decided to enroll in the local community college that fall. My dream was to become a high school speech communications teacher. Later that day, as I walked up the long flight of stairs to her office and knocked on her door, I felt excited. I just couldn't wait to tell her my decision!

The meeting started out exactly as I thought it would. We went over my grades and talked about my classes. Then she asked, "So, Tony, what are your plans after June?" With a big smile on my face, I told her my plan.

Her response was not the one I'd been anticipating all afternoon. She spoke in a mechanical tone, but her words pierced me like arrows: "Tony, I really don't think you're college material. Just keep working on your DJ business and forget about being a teacher."

I sat in my chair expressionless, paralyzed. Even now, years later, as I reflect on that conversation, I can recall the feeling of emptiness that invaded my soul that day, when my dreams were shaken by her careless words. I wonder how many other students were negatively affected by the "guidance" of this professional. Many times afterward, I wanted to visit her and allow my seething anger to burst into flames. I wanted to ask, "How could you have said such a thing to an impressionable high school student?" Wouldn't it be fun to carry my degrees with me and throw them on her desk?

Mrs. Harrison (not her real name) was a Dreamstealer. She did her best to convince me to put away my "immature and irresponsible" plans and settle for what she considered a practical, realistic vocation. I was instructed to put my imagination to rest, pay my last respects to my dream of becoming a teacher, and walk away forever. I needed to grow up.

More than twenty years have passed since that day. The wound from the guidance counselor's words is reduced to an almost indistinguishable scar. My anger is no longer directed at her, specifically, but I do feel alarmed and frustrated when I see parents, teachers, coaches, and others who refuse (or don't know how) to help young people discern the gifts inherent in their Design.

Dreamstealers possess varying degrees of power in our lives. Sometimes their injurious comments derail personal and professional trajectories, as their victims remain haunted by the stinging words of the assassins, sometimes for years, or for their entire lives. The raw nerves exposed by the Dreamstealers' arrows leave these individuals feeling helpless and hesitant to reveal their inner thoughts to another person ever again.

But sometimes, the injurious words hurt for a while but do little or no permanent damage. Why do some people react less severely than others to the words of a Dreamstealer? Why do some people grow stronger and more focused when their dreams are diminished by others, while others seem to be crushed?

I believe that familiarity with our *birthright gifts* adds to our resilience, enabling us to remain buoyant despite efforts (intentional and unintentional) to press us down. Further, understanding and celebrating our Design makes us less likely to act as a Dreamstealer in the lives of others. In fact, if we become infatuated with the joy of living by Design, we will likely encourage others to explore the clues to their own Design, and to craft their own *Personal Owner's Manual.*

Dreamstarters

"As human beings, our job in life is to help people realize how rare and valuable each one of us really is, that each of us has something that no one else has—or ever will have—something inside that is unique to all time. It's our job to encourage each other to discover that uniqueness and to provide ways of developing its expression." Fred Rogers

A skilled archaeologist may invest an entire lifetime in pursuit of a valuable artifact. He may sacrifice his time, money, and even his reputation on the slightest possibility that something of great worth lies below the sandy surface. Most of the time, his efforts promise little fortune, as he uncovers common pieces that can be found for sale at the market down the street. He dreams of uncovering treasures of inestimable worth. Such a discovery would compensate him for years of frustration and disappointment, and make up for the overpowering sense of defeat that has often beat him up when he tried to sleep at night.

Like the hopeful archaeologist, many of us long for the day when God will look down on us from his lofty view and point us in the direction of *wonder*ful riches. Maybe God does this by sending Dreamstarters into our lives.

What the Dreamstealer seeks to systematically dismantle within us, the Dreamstarter seeks to reinforce. Dreamstarters are people who point us away from our past failures, inadequacies, and other insecurities. They help us see ourselves not as we think we are, but as we can be. They help us cling to our childlike *wonder* and keep dreaming. Instead of criticizing us with admonishing words, often in the guise of helping us "face reality," they encourage us, as a mother robin does her young, to spread our wings and give it a try.

My high school guidance counselor, a trusted adult in a position of authority, almost convinced me I was not fit for college, so I chose to continue building my musical clientele through my DJ business. I was earning more than a hundred dollars an hour. It was *wonder*ful. I was essentially paid to play. The sounds of the bass pumping and the crowds cheering were music to my ears and money in my wallet. In the midst of what many would consider adolescent entrepreneurial success, however, I became aware of a gnawing emptiness inside. I wondered: Why am I doing so well, yet feeling so unhappy? God was speaking to me. He was exposing the inevitable void that would remain in my life if I continued to succumb to the advice of the Dreamstealer.

Late one night, a mysterious yet familiar sensation crept into my psyche. I had a mental image of running through my backyard by the old walnut tree, chasing after alien predators, and I felt invincible. The world of enchantment that I had abandoned so many years earlier was tugging at me. It was begging me to come out and play, and I was "it." The experience was almost euphoric in nature. Suddenly, I felt hopeful, even excited. That night, in an instant, the dust was removed from the handle of that old door to the place where magic happened. It was unlocked, and I walked in. I revisited my old love for reading, and did I ever read! Within a year, I had consumed nearly one hundred books. At that point, I was ready to meet my first *Dreamstarter.*

The Teacher with Extraordinary "Depth Perception"

Dr. Joe Byrd was young, passionate, and brilliant. I met him for the first time when I entered his classroom at King's Institute, a new college-level adult studies program in theology offered at a local church. I had learned about the program in the newspaper advertisement, and the class titles had invoked intrigue: Christian Doctrine and Hermeneutics.

So it was that, on a stormy Tuesday evening, I attended my first King's Institute class and met the teacher who would change my life. Dr. Byrd ("Joe") was a gifted communicator who knew how to illuminate with clarity the culture and message of a book alien to our own time and place. Never in my life had I been the recipient of such powerful teaching as his. I found myself keenly interested in the subject matter. I was devouring the material and wanted more.

One evening, Joe pulled me aside after class and asked if he could talk with me. What was he going to say? Was he pleased with my performance, or should I prepare myself for a familiar conversation about my suitability for school? My heart pounded. That's when Joe said, "Tony you are an exceptional student. Have you ever considered going away to college?"

His words, unlike those of my high school guidance counselor, infused me with life. To substantiate his suggestion, he gave examples of my ability to recall key concepts, historical movements, and ancient language references, and to synthesize and apply the information in meaningful ways. He quickly became my greatest advocate for a college education. In addition to providing me with an employment opportunity, he helped raise funds for me to attend college in pursuit of an undergraduate degree!

Twenty years later, I remain amazed and thankful for the gift of his influence and friendship. I have since completed bachelor's, master's, doctoral, and postdoctoral studies in theology, philosophy, leadership, law, and human resource management. I've attended several outstanding institutions, including Lee University, Regent University, Cornell University, University of Notre Dame, and UCLA.

What did Joe see in me that my guidance counselor did not? Mrs. Harrison perceived me to lack the aptitude and persistence to successfully complete a two-year community college program. Joe saw a young person hungry with questions and the compulsion to do the work necessary to complete a four-year degree and more. What Mrs. Harrison saw as arid ground, incapable of growing anything of consequence, Joe saw as rich and fertile, ready for the care and intellectual nurturing that only higher education could provide. Mrs. Harrison saw my GPA and my lack of college preparatory courses. Joe saw something else. The difference? Dreamstarters like Joe have a gift for seeing entelechies in others, while Dreamstealers like Mrs. Harrison suffer an impairment of depth perception. Where Dreamstarters see potential, Dreamstealers see only impossibility.

The Psychologist Who Saw a Person Instead of a Problem

In a TED Talk titled "Do Schools Kill Creativity?," Sir Ken Robinson tells the moving story of eight-year-old Gillian. Her teachers and parents were at their wit's end. Nothing was working. Day after day, Gillian struggled to pay attention and sit still in class. Each day, she was reprimanded for her disruptive behavior.

One day, Gillian's parents receive a disconcerting correspondence from the school, outlining the severity of Gillian's behavioral problems and demanding immediate action. The school recommended that she discontinue her studies and enroll in a "special school" that was better equipped to address students with severe psychological needs. Distraught, her parents scheduled an assessment with a psychologist.

At the psychologist's office, Gillian walked with her mother into a large, wood-paneled room filled with books. The doctor positioned himself far from Gillian and, for several minutes, directed his questions to her mother. The entire time, however, he watched Gillian intently. He thanked Gillian for her patience and asked her to remain seated while he and her mother spoke in the hallway. As they left the room, the psychologist turned on a radio and closed the door. Moments later, he directed Gillian's mother to a window that looked into the room where Gillian was waiting. There was Gillian, gliding across the floor, in sync with the music.

The psychologist told the exhausted mother, "Mrs. Lynne, your daughter is not sick; she is a dancer. Take her to dance school."

Years later, Gillian Lynne said her dance school was filled with kids just like her. Through her eventual partnership with Andrew Lloyd Webber, Gillian established herself as one of the world's greatest choreographers of all time, known especially for such classics as *The Phantom of the Opera* and *CATS*. In his book *The Element*, Robinson (2009) explains the pivotal role the psychologist played in the life of the dancer:

Little Gillian, the girl with the high-risk future, became known to the world as Gillian Lynne, one of the most accomplished choreographers of our time, someone who has brought pleasure to millions and earned millions of dollars. This happened because someone looked deep into her eyes—someone who had seen children like her before and knew how to read the signs. Someone else might have put her on medication and told her to calm down. But Gillian wasn't a problem child. She didn't need to go away to a special school. She just needed to be who she really was. (pp. 3-4)

As a little girl growing up in the 1920s, Gillian didn't know how to live according to her unique Design. She endured years of educational malnourishment and abuse by those tasked with her intellectual development. Though she likely faced a multitude of Dreamstealers, her mother cared for her so much that she sought an alternate perspective. This act of loving desperation resulted in Gillian meeting her first *Dreamstarter*. When her psychologist saw her dance, he sensed the stirring of her entelechies as her *birthright gifts* pleaded to be acknowledged and developed. Mrs. Lynne, likely relieved, dedicated herself to working with Gillian as they made important decisions that would lead Gillian toward her destiny. As Gillian's gifts matured, she redefined 20th century dance, forever changing her own life and touching the lives of others through her artistry.

Redefining Our Worldview

Even a cursory critique of American culture shines light on an alarming problem—an extreme preoccupation with human deficiencies, a persistent focus on "what's wrong" instead of "what's right" with ourselves and others. This thought pattern seems to have embedded itself into the collective American psyche. It has infiltrated our mental health system, our schools, other public and private organizations, and even our faith. We turn to self-help resources to fix our broken spirits and cosmetic treatments to make us look younger. We seem caught up in a never-ending quest to redefine the self according to the latest trends of societal acceptability.

America's prevailing makeover mentality encourages an attitude of extreme personal dissatisfaction. Numerous popular television shows tug at our gnawing sense of incompleteness by suggesting it can be alleviated by modifying one's appearance and lifestyle. In this worldview, people are essentially problems to be solved. Interestingly, the solution to the problem is elusive, as societal trends are constantly in flux. Keeping up with the Joneses— oops, I mean the Kardashians—thus becomes an exercise in frustration, with no end in sight.

Sadly, vain attempts to construct a "proper" or "popular" self distract us from the possibility of knowing and appreciating our *true* selves, as our external focus stifles individuality. As a result, we live and lead our lives critically disengaged from our soul. It's no wonder that professional burnout is on the rise. Investing 40-plus hours a week doing work that's not related to our vocation or calling tends to suffocate rather than sustain, to suppress instead of stimulate. Detachment kills drive.

To make matters worse, the kinetic American lifestyle keeps us from hitting the pause button, reflecting on our situation, adjusting our approach, and moving toward self-realization. Consequently, Americans drift from one job to the next, from one new experience to another, seeking something to satisfy a thirsty soul.

The preoccupation with human deficits extends beyond popular culture. Numerous academic and professional disciplines are based on the philosophy that people need to be "fixed." For example:

- **Education**: Students are blank slates (tabula rasa) on which knowledge must be written. They possess little in the way of innate knowledge or predispositions. Pedagogy (the art of teaching) is undifferentiated, based on the assumption that "what works for one will work for all."

- **Leadership**: People and organizations are problems to be solved.

- **Medicine and psychology**: Health is a matter of diagnosing and remediating psychosis or disease. There is little emphasis on prevention, or holistic approaches.

- **Religion**: The depraved and dark aspects of human nature are strongly emphasized, and aspects of goodness and light are ignored.

Across the disciplines, an obsession with deficits permeates the way we view ourselves. We invest in countless measures to re-create or redefine ourselves according to external standards of acceptability. We strive to compensate for our deficits, real or imagined, but remain ill-equipped to consider our Design. Instead of developing a *Personal Owner's Manual* based on our Design, and conforming our behaviors to its specifications, we're distracted, in a state of existential disarray. We yearn for something, but can't put our finger on exactly what it is. Our incessant experimentalism has little meaning. Our unique gifts beg to be acknowledged, developed, and used, but their cry goes unheard amidst a flurry of activity and busyness.

I had the rare privilege of sitting in the classroom of Dr. Chip Anderson, a renowned psychologist and educator at UCLA and Azusa Pacific University, shortly before he died. In concert with his own mentor, Don Clifton, Dr. Anderson was a pioneer in the field of human potentiality, the "strengths movement." He told his students that we spend the vast majority of our lives attempting to fix ourselves. We become adequate in much but excellent at nothing. He believed that until a person discovers, affirms, develops, and strategically applies his or her strengths, that person will remain restless and without a viable purpose.

As a theist, Dr. Anderson believed attentiveness to one's giftedness was perhaps the greatest expression of worship a human can offer to the Divine. Without reservation, he believed one's existence within a particular time and place to be divinely inspired. Strengths, he said, can act as a creative roadmap, pointing us toward our destinies. He argued that strengths within the wrong context would repeatedly "beat us up." For example, my disposition toward invention means I flourish in situations where I'm required to consider new alternative ways to think and act. If I find myself within an environment that rewards sustainability alone, doing things as they have always been done, I quickly lose interest, and my performance falters.

Though it's not wise to ignore our weaknesses completely, we should invest only limited time and resources in those areas, enough to be functional. The majority of our investment should be directed toward our strengths (our Design).

A few years ago, my father remarked that had he known how much he would enjoy playing music professionally, he would have left his factory job years earlier and found a way to do what he was best at all the time. "For the first time in my life," he told me, "I'm having fun!" Considering the wonder of our Design, our giftedness is truly remarkable. Our individuality is not to be squandered by or subjugated to popular opinion, but explored and refined.

Chapter Three will challenge readers to embrace the journey of leading by Design. It's not devoted to supervising others, though many of its principles could be applied toward that end. Rather, it explores the innumerable benefits and challenges of leading *oneself* as a prerequisite to leading others. The focus is not outward but inward, as we consider what's beautiful (and not so beautiful) about ourselves.

Notes

*Record memories, insights, and epiphanies here
so that you can refer to them later.*

Notes

Notes

Chapter Three: Leading by Design

"In the morning when thou risest unwillingly, let this thought be present—I am rising to the work of a human being. Why then am I dissatisfied if I am going to do the things for which I exist and for which I was brought into the world? Or have I been made for this, to lie in the bedclothes and keep myself warm? But this is more pleasant. Dost thou exist then to take thy pleasure, and not all for action or exertion? Dost thou not see the little plants, the little birds, the ants, the spiders, the bees working together to put in order their several parts of the universe? And art thou unwilling to do the work of a human being, and dost thou not make haste to do that which is according to thy nature?" Marcus Aurelius

"One of the keys to any possible happiness in work must be the little self-knowledge it takes to know what we desire in life, how we are made, and how we belong to the rest of the world." David Whyte

"A new leadership is needed for new times, but it will not come from finding new and more wily ways to manipulate the external world. It will come as we who lead find the courage to take an inner journey toward both our shadows and our light—a journey, that faithfully pursued will take us beyond ourselves to become healers of a wounded world." Parker Palmer

The moment we enter the world, we start learning. Through our senses, we absorb information about our new surroundings and begin the process of meaning-making. The newness of everything produces wonder, though we don't yet have the language to describe our response. As young children, we envision ourselves conquering the world and taking our place at the center of its axis, perhaps by exploring outer space, or discovering a cure for an epidemic, or otherwise making our mark.

Formal schooling brings new knowledge and experiences—but if the educational environment is rigid and impersonal, it can be an unsuitable incubator for our lofty goals. If education encourages us to seek approval and guidance only from external sources, but denies or represses the qualities that make us unique (our Design), we might embark on a journey toward conformity. When that happens, we risk accepting others' conclusions about "what it all means" instead of creating our own meanings. Without the internal compass of self-knowledge to guide our choices, trial and error shape our pursuit of that for which we have no name. As time passes, we lose sight of exciting possibilities on the horizon, keep our heads down, and plod paths that lead us ever farther from choices and experiences that might bring us happiness.

Pascal presented a somber account of the life experienced by those who do not see themselves and their world with a sense of wonder and passion. He writes, "Nothing is so insufferable to man as to be completely at rest, without passions, without busyness, without diversion, without effort. Then he feels his nothingness, his forlornness, his insufficiency, his weakness, his emptiness" (in *Thoughts,* Section II, Part 131, translated by Trotter, 1910). In *The Spirit of the Disciplines,* philosopher Dallas Willard describes the stagnation that can occur in individuals who don't practice intentional living: "Some persons indeed try to abdicate their life, disown their spontaneity, seek security by 'conforming' to what is outside of them. But they don't actually escape life or their responsibility for it. They only succeed in appearing 'wooden,' unlively. We may know what to expect from them, but we have as little delight in them as they do in themselves."

For nearly ten years, my friend and former colleague Doug Walters and I have volunteered our time as instructors in a leadership development academy for emerging to mid-level professionals. We deliver interactive presentations on discovering and developing strengths, increasing emotional intelligence, and learning how to lead others. Each year, without fail, a handful of participants asks to speak with us privately afterwards. Many say they feel empty inside when they go to their jobs, and describe a transactional relationship with their work. They show up, do what is required, go home, receive pay, and then do it all over again. They share sobering stories of feeling trapped in their jobs. They seek counsel on how to respond to the persistent, nagging awareness that they were meant for something more, something that inspires wonder, something that is challenging yet feels natural.

Often these leaders-in-training are surprised to hear that we don't have the answers they seek, though we can tell them where to look—not in the business section of the local bookstore, but within themselves. We point them toward the discovery of their Design. Further, we encourage them to develop the equivalent of a *Personal Owner's Manual* to help them live and lead in harmony with their Design. Self-awareness is the prerequisite to intentional living (living by Design), which in turn energizes our soul and diminishes the likelihood of feeling wooden or hollow, in desperate need of a weekend reprieve or some other form of escape.

Telling emerging leaders to "write their own instruction manual" instead of purchasing a ready-made formula for professional success might seem like a tall order. This is not to say that books on leadership and management are worthless. On the contrary, studying and applying best practices makes a great deal of sense.

Certainly, it's worthwhile to learn strategies for motivating employees to reach their full potential through coaching, creative incentivizing, or implementing new organizational structures. Nearly all "prescriptions" for leadership, however, focus primarily on the relationship of leader and follower.

My study of leadership reveals a glaring void: Seldom are leaders encouraged to examine their inner lives. Yet the complex nature of individuals' internal constitution affects the quality of their leadership. The baggage that many bring with them to the workplace is barely manageable, yet rarely considered as a relevant factor in leadership success.

The Ascent Toward Authenticity

> *"The only true joy on earth is to escape from the prison of our own false self."* Thomas Merton

> *"You find peace not by rearranging the circumstances of your life, but by realizing who you are at the deepest level."* Thomas Merton

It is a mundane existence for the man in the cave. His presence on this planet is known to none but the shadows that occasionally invade his solitude. Mobility restricted insofar as his chains allow, the man lies transfixed by the porosity of the wall before him. He slowly glides his rough, calloused hand across the cool rivulets of water that appear and disappear according to a mysterious rhythm that he can almost forecast.

His is a life of predictability. This black-and-white, shadowy, two-dimensional world affords him an existence free from the unexpected. Every day is the same inside the walls of this cavernous prison. The safety of this confine prompts no fantasy of a better life, as even its slightest consideration could arouse trepidation. This is all he knows—all he has ever known. To inhale deeply without detecting the sweet, musty aroma of decay would certainly invoke panic in this man.

Imagine how the man feels when, upon waking, he finds the chains that held him tight for so long are suddenly gone. He yearns for their embrace as an infant does his security blanket. He cries out in agony at the loss of his chains. His heart races as his atrophied limbs, awakened from years of dormancy, begin the unnatural task of miniscule movement.

Yet despite his duress, something compels him to lift his head. What he sees high above the walls of his home causes him to retreat into the comfort of the shadows. A pinprick of light pierces the blanket of darkness in which he is wrapped, and the man experiences an odd sensation as his fear duals with an even greater force—curiosity. Fumbling around like a toddler taking his first steps, the man resolves to ascend the rocky wall in pursuit of the light.

Every arduous movement begs a new question: *Who am I? Where did I come from? Is there more?*

Midway up the wall, the man stops to rest and gauge his progress. Compelled to look up once again, he quickly closes his eyes. What a strange feeling! He looks down from whence he came, momentarily contemplating a return to his known universe. Propelled by an unfamiliar yet strangely welcome compulsion to explore, the man reengages his climb toward the light.

Upon reaching the very summit of his prison, the man summons what remains of his strength, pulls himself up and out, and stands in the open air. He is immediately disoriented by the blinding light, and by the strange sounds and smells. He surrenders to his knees. As he hesitantly reopens his eyes, he finds himself overwhelmed by competing emotions. Unveiled before him is a breathtaking landscape in all its vivid color, tonality, and dimensionality. He cautiously does a 360-degree turn, looking all around him, and then at himself. He stares at his limbs, at his feet and hands, and notices their finite details, illuminated for the first time.

Overcome, the man begins to cry. His predicament prompts tears of despair, followed by tears of joy. Had his chains been real or imagined? Had this strange, new world always existed? What opportunities awaited him in this life outside the cave? Where shall he begin exploring first?

At once he recognizes that all he had ever believed to be true about himself and his universe had been severely distorted by his limited perspective while in the cave. This new idea is confirmed as his attention is seized by the playfulness of his own large, dysmorphic shadow moving on the ground before him. "Why, this shadow isn't really me," he thinks to himself. "In fact, it looks very little like me." He recalls investing a lifetime watching the shadows in his dark cave.

Though physically and emotionally spent, he knows, deep within his constitution, that the frightening climb was worth every ounce of exertion. For the first time in his life, he knows the truth.

He is free.

###

Much creative extrapolation from Plato's *Allegory of the Cave* is evident in the above version of this timeless narrative. However, even 2,500 years removed from its initial telling, many lessons remain worthy of consideration. Unaware of our Design, many of us, like the man in the cave, find ourselves trapped within the confines of familiarity. Whether restrained "far below" because of the caustic words of a Dreamstealer, or reticent to face our greatest fears, we extend only a shadowy image of ourselves toward those around us.

Leading by *Design* requires us to assess ourselves in light of our surroundings and to sever any chains that keep us from our journey of discovery. While we may not always like what the light reveals, its sanitizing warmth helps expose our true selves, and illuminates a vast world in which we can run free.

In his classic poem, *Please Hear What I'm Not Saying*, Charles C. Finn describes the inner turmoil everyone faces to authentically know and be known by others. Removing the familiar facades that constrict our Design is one of the greatest gifts we can offer ourselves and the world.

Please Hear What I'm Not Saying

Don't be fooled by me.
Don't be fooled by the face I wear
for I wear a mask, a thousand masks,
masks that I'm afraid to take off,
and none of them is me.
Pretending is an art that's second nature with me,
but don't be fooled,
for God's sake don't be fooled.
I give you the impression that I'm secure,

that all is sunny and unruffled with me, within as well as without,
that confidence is my name and coolness my game,
that the water's calm and I'm in command
and that I need no one,
but don't believe me.
My surface may seem smooth but my surface is my mask,
ever-varying and ever-concealing.
Beneath lies no complacence.
Beneath lies confusion, and fear, and aloneness.
But I hide this. I don't want anybody to know it.
I panic at the thought of my weakness exposed.
That's why I frantically create a mask to hide behind,
a nonchalant sophisticated facade,
to help me pretend,
to shield me from the glance that knows.
But such a glance is precisely my salvation, my only hope,
and I know it.
That is, if it's followed by acceptance,
if it's followed by love.
It's the only thing that can liberate me from myself,
from my own self-built prison walls,
from the barriers I so painstakingly erect.
It's the only thing that will assure me
of what I can't assure myself,
that I'm really worth something.
But I don't tell you this. I don't dare to, I'm afraid to.
I'm afraid your glance will not be followed by acceptance,
will not be followed by love.
I'm afraid you'll think less of me,
that you'll laugh, and your laugh would kill me.
I'm afraid that deep-down I'm nothing
and that you will see this and reject me.
So I play my game, my desperate pretending game,
with a facade of assurance without
and a trembling child within.
So begins the glittering but empty parade of masks,

and my life becomes a front.
I idly chatter to you in the suave tones of surface talk.
I tell you everything that's really nothing,
and nothing of what's everything,
of what's crying within me.
So when I'm going through my routine
do not be fooled by what I'm saying.
Please listen carefully and try to hear what I'm not saying,
what I'd like to be able to say,
what for survival I need to say,
but what I can't say.
I don't like hiding.
I don't like playing superficial phony games.
I want to stop playing them.
I want to be genuine and spontaneous and me
but you've got to help me.
You've got to hold out your hand
even when that's the last thing I seem to want.
Only you can wipe away from my eyes
the blank stare of the breathing dead.
Only you can call me into aliveness.
Each time you're kind, and gentle, and encouraging,
each time you try to understand because you really care,
my heart begins to grow wings—
very small wings,
very feeble wings,
but wings!
With your power to touch me into feeling
you can breathe life into me.
I want you to know that.
I want you to know how important you are to me,
how you can be a creator—an honest-to-God creator—
of the person that is me
if you choose to.
You alone can break down the wall behind which I tremble,
you alone can remove my mask,

you alone can release me from my shadow-world of panic,
from my lonely prison,
if you choose to.
Please choose to.
Do not pass me by.
It will not be easy for you.
A long conviction of worthlessness builds strong walls.
The nearer you approach to me the blinder I may strike back.
It's irrational, but despite what the books say about man
often I am irrational.
I fight against the very thing I cry out for.
But I am told that love is stronger than strong walls
and in this lies my hope.
Please try to beat down those walls
with firm hands but with gentle hands
for a child is very sensitive.
Who am I, you may wonder?
I am someone you know very well.
For I am every man you meet
and I am every woman you meet.

Charles C. Finn's poem is powerful because it awakens readers to their inner life, where the voice of the true self can be heard.

The remainder of this chapter presents three key components of the inner life of a leader: introspection, integration, and intervention. Failure to execute these internal strategies can keep us "in the cave" and render external leadership strategies ineffective, even if those strategies have succeeded elsewhere. To paraphrase a well-known saying, "Leader, lead thyself."

Introspection

"Even though 'knowing oneself' may not involve as strenuous a quest for a business leader as it does for a philosopher, it is still an arduous task. It means reflecting seriously on one's own experience, asking: What are the things that matter most to me? Who are the people I admire most? What kind of person do I definitely not want to be? What are the values I would not compromise under any circumstance?" Mihaly Csikszentmihalyi

"When I discover who I am, I'll be free." Ralph Ellison, *Invisible Man*

"Each man had only one genuine vocation—to find the way to himself.... His task was to discover his own destiny—not an arbitrary one—and to live it out wholly and resolutely within himself. Everything else was only a would-be existence, an attempt at evasion, a flight back to the ideals of the masses, conformity and fear of one's own inwardness." Hermann Hesse

"It is often the case that many false paths, usually presented by the ego, must be tried and put aside before our real work, our real mission, may be discovered." David Ulrich

Leading Naked: The Costly Consequences of Solipsism

sol·ip·sism /ˈsälipˌsizəm/ — The view or theory that the self is all that can be known to exist.

In one of the most acclaimed children's stories of all time, Hans Christian Andersen (1873) shows what can happen when leaders become so inebriated by the effects of power and position that they become oblivious to the world around them. *The Emperor's*

New Clothes portrays an indulgent, narcissistic leader who exists within a self-contrived reality, devoid of truth. His raison d'être ("reason for being") is to be admired by others. He foolishly employs two "tailors" to make a magnificent garment for him as he seeks the approval and affection of the masses. The con artists say the cloth of the garment is "invisible to anyone who is too stupid and incompetent to appreciate its quality." The emperor, of course, can't actually see his new garment, since it doesn't exist, and neither can anyone else. Yet when he "wears" it during a public processional, the onlookers reinforce the emperor's psychosis by saying how exquisite it is. This manufactured reality is challenged when a small child innocently asks why the emperor is naked. The crowd responds, "The boy is right! The emperor is naked! It's true." The absurdity of the situation becomes a topic of discussion throughout the kingdom.

How can leaders (or followers) avoid giving in to the intoxicating effects of status? They can start by understanding the following about human nature: When the facts deviate from our idea of what's "normal" or expected, we tend to overlook or skew the facts to make them fit our preconceived notion of "what is." Our attempts to understand and communicate "what is" are colored by the lenses of our personalities, preferences, and presuppositions.

Throughout my life, I've heard parents, teachers, pastors, and others talk about "the truth." Many, especially within the ecclesiastical context, speak with authority and passion. All truth claims are subject to an epistemological system—beliefs about the nature, limits, and validity of knowledge. While I embrace the existence of objective truth, I'm also aware that each person's interpretation of the truth is subjective because we all have "baggage" that colors our perspective. For example, race, religion, gender, socio-economic status, education, geographical origin, and personal tragedies shape one's worldview and affects one's perspective on "what is." It's impossible to separate our baggage from our inquiry. So when we make truth claims, especially in the presence of others, it's important that we consider how our worldview impacts the way we acquire, process, and disseminate knowledge.

One thing that made me want to study organizational leadership at the doctoral level was my need to make sense of the disturbing behaviors that certain leaders exhibited. I wondered: What qualities are essential for one to be identified by others as a promising leader? To what extent does one's personal disposition inform leadership decisions? Within the context of religion, what is the relationship of one's personality to one's overall conception of the Almighty?

In college, I was curious about the degree to which the revelations of a religious leader were influenced by the disposition of the messenger. While I accept the tenets of organic inspiration (the idea that the message of God is made manifest through the personality and abilities of a human author), I also think that one's personality influences the person's understanding and interpretation of the will of God. As we seek to align ourselves with truth, we must be aware that there's no way for us to free ourselves completely from subjective constraints such as personality, human relationships, and experiences. We must acknowledge the presence of these factors; consider the ways they influence our thinking; and move forward with our inquiry. One of the most important tools for exposing the subjective elements that shape our viewpoints is the dialectical process, or human interaction. It is within the presence of community that we are able to work together to unravel complexities and form conclusions.

Some leaders, however, choose to restrict or filter their engagement with others in order to minimize scrutiny. Such leaders surround themselves with people who constantly affirm the leader's viewpoint. While A is occurring in the organization, the leader chooses to reside in an alternate universe that embraces B as reality. This alternate universe, which closely resembles the one in Andersen's *The Emperor's New Clothes*, is primarily self-referential. I call this common phenomenon "organizational solipsism."

Solipsism is a philosophical term that describes a detached, self-centered worldview in which all things are created by the observer. Nothing exists outside of this cognitive exercise. An example is Andersen's emperor—a person in authority who held a self-generated, self-moderated, insular worldview. The authority's perspective on "what is" may be externally fueled by other stakeholders in an organization who believe that by seeking favor with the leader, their own agendas may be advanced. This form of solipsism can act as a fast-spreading contagion within an organization as individuals acquiesce to the perspective of the leader. It can put the health of the organization in jeopardy, as the organization becomes disconnected from reality. Andersen alludes to such situations in his fairy tale as he describes the inner struggles of a messenger who sees what others deny—that the emperor is naked. In the end, the messenger caved in and, in Andersen's words, "praised the stuff he could not see, and declared that he was delighted with both colors and patterns."

Several years ago, my scholarly interest in leadership studies was piqued while working at a college wherein the president was persistently praised for the fact that the organization was growing. The press, members of the board, and community leaders cited the spike in student enrollment and the expansion of the physical campus as compelling indicators of presidential success. While brick and mortar were transformed into numerous buildings, however, many student and faculty lives were adversely affected. The alternate universe in which the president resided did not acknowledge the alarmingly low faculty morale. The shiny veneer of sacred terminology (words such as *mission, calling,* and *service*) concealed the use of paranoia as a control mechanism, putrefying beneath the surface. Divergent viewpoints offered in the spirit of sincerity and collegiality were quickly extinguished and categorized as insubordination and intolerable. Decisions were made on a regular basis that diminished the value of human capital and perpetuated a crippling cynicism and blatant distrust within the culture. Students and staff members were reluctant to express their concerns for fear of losing scholarships or jobs. In this story, the emperor and his courtiers tried to manage public opinion outside of the campus by emphasizing the growth of the kingdom and the remarkable loyalty of the kingdom's inhabitants to their leader.

Every leader is capable of succumbing to the temptation of organizational solipsism. The unhealthy synergy of ambition, personal insecurities, mental illness (in some cases), and the blind loyalty of followers can lead individuals down the path of untruth, even if they have the best of intentions. History is replete with examples of leaders who achieved remarkable success, but at a cost. The extermination of human populations, the loss of billions of dollars through dubious financial practices, and countless other incidents reveal emperors and courtiers wearing no clothes—in other words, inhabiting a lie.

Though the allure of creating an alternate universe in which the self reigns supreme is compelling, the casualties that may be incurred along the way make it a deplorable course of action. Leaders, no matter how smart, skilled or successful, must always be aware that the baggage they carry can have a marked impact on an organization, its staff, and those the organization serves. Effective leaders are highly aware of their humanness, and they establish practices to reinforce accountability and the pursuit of what's real.

Sometimes, leaders might worry that introspection is a selfish or self-indulgent act. Nothing could be further from the truth. Since ancient times, understanding the complexity of the self has been lauded as a worthwhile and necessary aspiration. In *Phaedrus*, Plato writes, "I must first know myself, as the Delphian inscription says. To be curious about that which is not my concern, while I am still in ignorance of my own self, would be ridiculous.... Am I a monster more complicated and swollen with passion than the serpent Typhon, or a creature of a gentler and simpler sort, to whom nature has given a diviner and lowlier destiny?" (translated by Yunis, 2009).

Much harmful leadership behavior has its origin on the playground, long ago, when an unkind word was spoken, a classmate refused to play, or a bully pummeled the child's face. Old wounds, unattended, fester over time and cause irreparable harm to others decades later. Effective leaders understand their vulnerabilities. Remember: hurting people hurt others.

Leading by Design requires that we not only embrace our unique giftedness but also, through solitary and communal introspection, examine and acknowledge our own liabilities. No one should have to tolerate our bad behavior. Every out-of-control leader who acts recklessly or berates others could curb those bad behaviors— if they understood their own vulnerabilities, acknowledged their humanness, and learned compassionate restraint. Gaining awareness in this area requires introspection.

Introspection may seem incompatible with busyness, as it requires time and concerted effort. However, no one can afford *not* to invest in self-awareness. Humans are beautifully and frighteningly complex, capable of bringing joy to others, or inflicting pain on them. When leaders invest in understanding both the good and not-so-good aspects of their Design, people and organizations will benefit.

Leader: Know and Control Thyself

I'm fortunate to have had the opportunity to work in a variety of for-profit corporations and nonprofit organizations, including universities and churches. From the outside, one might assume that vast differences exist between such entities. Clearly, each contains its own set of processes and peculiarities. For the most part, however, they are more alike than different. Organizations of all kinds consist of people, and people behave similarly.

My work as a consultant has brought me in close proximity to leaders who struggle to keep their organizations viable as they face a barrage of obstacles, such as shifting economic conditions and a disengaged or underperforming workforce. A consultant generally conducts an organizational assessment to better understand what's keeping the organization from success. It doesn't take long to identify external threats (e.g., a shrewd competitor gobbling up the market) or internal issues (e.g., a department manager who's not a team player). More often than not, however, the real problem lies elsewhere—at the very top of the organizational chart. Whether the leader is a university president, chief executive officer, physician, or church pastor, that person's unrestrained ego is often the root cause of organizational decline. Bad behavior has been tolerated for various reasons, poor decisions have been made, and over time, the causalities have piled up: the organization is now in crisis.

All leaders are susceptible to the intoxicating effects of power and position. Even those with the most heavenly of ambitions must regularly assess their actions to make sure they are not driven by unbecoming, primal impulses. Religious leaders who refrain from introspection can easily misappropriate the Divine for a convoluted mix of personal insecurities, paranoia, greed, jealousy, and antagonism toward others. No level of busyness exists in which a leader should be precluded from introspection.

Leaders must guard against assuming that their baggage belongs in the workplace. Excessive sharing or venting by a leader can have a negative effect on the productivity of other employees—especially if they find themselves serving as surrogate counselors to their supervisors who, in the name of friendship, mistake the workplace for a counseling clinic. Or leaders who feel they have little control over their own circumstances might try to exert control by ensuring that those around them feel equally miserable. Either way, the leader's baggage is being dumped on others and causing harm.

More benign in intent but equally harmful is the common practice of becoming so engrossed in the importance of a particular task or timeline that the resulting stress becomes an excuse for bad behavior. The leader might say, "I always become a _____ when a deadline nears." This person might expect or ask others to forgive such episodic craziness. Henry Cloud (2013), author *of Boundaries for Leaders,* encourages leaders to control their behavior. He writes,

> Too many times leaders, in the absence of someone looking over their shoulder, allow the reality of the mission or the circumstances to lead and to shape them. They get into a reactive mode, always responding to

external forces and problems, and quickly losing sight of their larger role and purpose. The crush of urgent crises, to-do lists, squeaky wheel people, and distracting details takes over. It can feel very much like it is a war "out there" that requires shooting and ducking every waking hour of the day. In this flurry of activity, too many leaders forget that they also need to manage themselves, since no one else is doing it; they fail to put into place key boundaries of self-leadership that the sheer volume of work and responsibilities can obscure. (p. 198)

Leading by Design requires a commitment to contemplation. Because we are fallible beings, however, any kind of scrutiny, whether from ourselves or from others, can beget fear. When we look inside ourselves, what we find may not always be pleasant. Thomas Merton writes, "Let no one hope to find in contemplation an escape from conflict, from anguish or from doubt. On the contrary, the deep inexpressible certitude of the contemplative experience awakens a tragic anguish and opens many questions in the depths of the heart like wounds that cannot stop bleeding" (p. 12). Examining ourselves will reveal much that may seem disheartening.

The inner life of a leader can be a lonely and sometimes painful place. However, there is great value in exploring factors that can impede the beauty of our Design. Painful revelations need not be addressed all at once; they can be addressed over time. As leaders, the more that we invest in introspection, acknowledge our liabilities, and seek wholeness, the better positioned we are to make a positive impact on those we are privileged to serve—and to ensure that our liabilities don't creep into our relationships or our organizations.

Integration

> *"I have a picture, a sort of general theory of the universe in my mind that I have built up over the decades. If I read an article, or hear someone give a seminar talk, or in some other way get some piece of information about science that I hadn't had before, I ask myself: 'How does that fit into my picture of the universe?' and if it doesn't fit, I ask: Why doesn't it fit in?"* Linus Pauling, Nobel Prize winner, as quoted in Csikszentmihalyi, 2003

If it was my mother's goal to ensure that learning become an inexorable compulsion when she drove me to story hour at the library week after week, she certainly succeeded. I cannot recall any particular season of my childhood or adult life in which I was not pursuing answers to a series of nagging questions. As an adult, I established a pattern of seeking a formal degree or credential, taking a short break, then starting the process all over again.

Thanks to Dr. Joe Byrd's advocacy, coupled with my unyielding persistence, I was most fortunate to be hired as a Residence Director in a freshman residence hall after I completed my undergraduate degree at Lee University. This exciting, full-time opportunity provided me the experience of developing several student leaders, who in turn served two hundred residents through peer mentoring, event planning, and direct assistance in connecting to opportunities across the university. In addition to receiving a monetary stipend and university housing (within the residence hall), I received a full tuition benefit toward the pursuit of a master's degree.

At that time, the university had recently publicized a new, somewhat experimental graduate program in liberal arts that drew interest from many recent graduates and adult learners who sought a nontraditional approach to learning. While most students attend college to pursue a specialized degree as a prerequisite to a specific career, the Master of Liberal Arts degree was created in response to the disciplinary isolationism plaguing many postsecondary programs worldwide. A quick review of the program description and a sample syllabus for the first course ("The Great Questions") left little doubt that this was the master's program for me!

The first course was team-taught by a philosopher/theologian and a sociologist. Both gentlemen, lauded as leaders in their fields, presented a distinct yet coherent analysis of humanity's most profound existential questions. Students were required to engage in thoughtful dialogue that demonstrated mastery of the assigned reading, integration of multiple disciplines, and meaningful application to the present-day context. I remember being unable to sleep following that first night class. My mind raced, captivated by a single question: *Why isn't all learning like this?* The interdisciplinary approach made so much sense to me! I saw how the disciplines were complementary, working together to paint a complete, integrative picture of the world.

Opportunities for interdisciplinary learning are rare. Usually, students are conditioned to consider only the pragmatic aspects of their learning. They learn to think, behave, and respond to problems within the confines of whatever discipline they study. Yet the problems people encounter in life and at work are multifaceted, and they demand more cognitive power than an interrogative "groupthink" session can produce. Interdisciplinary learning helps students avoid compartmentalization as they embrace diverse viewpoints and methodologies in the quest for truth.

The trend toward compartmentalization is not limited to education. When we turn on the television or browse the web, marketers inundate us with if/then propositions: If you acquire the right outfit, car, job, or technology, then you will be content. When we accept these persuasive promises as true, and blindly obey the command to pursue them, we ignore our multidimensional natures and sabotage our efforts to find purpose and joy. Humans are not merely consumers in search of "some new thing." Consider the various facets of being human:

Multidimensional Nature of a Person

1. Spiritual/Ethical (our conscience, our criterion for determining right and wrong, our engagement with the Transcendent)
2. Physical (our bodies, health, and fitness)
3. Vocational (our calling, our *raison d'être*—reason for existence)
4. Relational (one of our most primal needs: family, friends, companionship)
5. Educational (humans possess an innate need to know, to inquire, to learn)
6. Playful (regardless of age, finding opportunities for fun keeps us young)
7. Material (the things we purchase or craft for our pleasure)

My graduate program framed the pursuit of truth as multidimensional. Its interdisciplinary approach didn't ask students to use only one lens or paradigm to find answers to life's most perplexing questions. It acknowledged that human beings are complex creatures who thrive when all aspects of our Design are affirmed and integrated. For each individual, a wonderful story eagerly waits to be written. Introspection and integration prepare us to write our stories—but making a meaningful difference in the world requires that we, as leaders, take up the pen and write.

Intervention

> *"We are all born with a bundle of aptitudes, most of which we are not even aware of having. According to some, the highest level of happiness—self-actualization—is being able to express all the potentialities inherent in the organism. It is as if evolution has built a safety device in our nervous system that allows us to experience full happiness only when we are living at 100 percent—when we are fully using the physical and mental equipment we have been given. This mechanism would ensure that after all our other needs were taken care of, we would still seek to use the full complement of our talents, thereby making it possible not just to preserve the status quo, but also to innovate and grow."* Mihaly Csikszentmihalyi

A healthy community is composed of a diverse group of individuals willing to invest themselves in the realization of a shared vision for the future. How tragic it is when a member of the community chooses to keep his or her gift contained. This selfish act creates a vacuum that is impossible to fill, as no other person has precisely the same Design. We are the conservator of our Design, which means we preserve it not by keeping it concealed, but by developing our birthright gifts and using them for the greater good. Because many of us will devote the vast majority of our waking hours to work, it's worth asking: What can we do to ensure that our professional activities are commensurate with our Design?

Orientation Is Everything

I have been most fortunate to travel across the globe, to many countries in Europe, Africa, the Americas, and Asia. Some of these adventures were for work or school, while others were for pleasure. Regardless of the nature of the travel, or the political and socioeconomic proclivities of the region, I've often found myself immersed in conversations about the role of work and whether happiness in one's job should be a priority. Is work merely a means to survival? What does one's orientation to work say about him or her? If one views his or her employment as a job versus a career versus a calling, does that matter? Why do people drift from one job to another so often? Is it simply a generational attribute of the Millennials, who are now infiltrating the workplace? Is a life of professional transience the new norm? Could it be motivated by a yearning for a job or place or team that feels like "home"? Can personal and professional restlessness be curbed when we discover how to live and lead by Design?

My doctoral dissertation examined the relationship of "meaning in life" to burnout in second- and third-tier leaders within commerce, education, and government. I wanted to know whether a prevailing purposefulness played a role in the degree to which one might encounter the debilitating symptoms of burnout. Connected to this query was an examination of the degree to which one's orientation to work might be a contributing factor to meaning in life, and affect one's propensity for burnout.

Drawing upon the excellent work of Amy Wrzesniewski, I asked the participants in my study whether they viewed their employment as a job, career, or calling. A brief definition was attached to each of these terms. Additionally, participants completed the Meaning in Life Questionnaire (MLQ) and the Maslach Burnout Inventory (MBI). Through correlational analysis, it was determined that those who ranked high in meaning in life, and identified their employment as a calling rather than a career or a job, showed the least likelihood of exhibiting the three symptoms of burnout: emotional exhaustion, cynicism, and diminished professional efficacy.

Robert Bellah and colleagues (1985) indicated that within the first orientation, people who view work as a job spend their time "focusing on the material benefits of work to the relative exclusion of other kinds of meaning and fulfillment. The work is simply a means to a financial end that allows people to enjoy their time away from work. Usually, the interests and ambitions of those with Jobs are expressed outside of the domain of work and involve hobbies and other interests" (p. 66).

In contrast, those who embrace work as a calling "work not for financial rewards or for advancement but for the fulfillment that doing the work brings. In callings, the work is an end in itself and is associated with the belief that the work makes the world a better place" (Wrzesniewski et al., p. 22). Leading by Design enhances our perceived value of our work. Channeling our Design into a calling solidifies our identity internally and among those around us. Michael Pratt and Blake Ashforth (2003) write,

> We believe that practices that best typify meaningfulness in working are those that nurture callings. When one's work is a calling, it is seen as socially valuable—an end in itself—involving activities that may, but need not be pleasurable. Callings have also been associated with expressing one's "authentic self" in what one does. When you answer your calling, you become the person that only you can be. As such, callings involve role, identity, and meaningfulness. (p. 320)

Preventing Burnout

Doing a job day after day, devoid of engagement, makes us ideal candidates for burnout. Burnout has been identified as the greatest occupational hazard of the 21st century because of its consequential physical and emotional distress, related workplace absenteeism, and detachment from the job—translating into billions of dollars in lost revenue.

Wilmar Schaufeli and Dirk Enzmann (1998) defined the burnout metaphor as "a persistent, negative, work-related state of mind in 'normal' individuals that is primarily characterized by exhaustion, which is accompanied by distress, a state of reduced effectiveness, decreased motivation, and the development of dysfunctional attitudes and behaviors at work. This psychological condition develops gradually but may remain unnoticed for a long time by the individual involved. It results from a misfit between intentions and reality in the job. Often burnout is self-perpetuating because of inadequate coping strategies that are associated with the syndrome" (p. 36).

Burnout is inevitable when we make professional choices without consulting our Design. Issues of "person-job-fit" slowly atrophy our energy and efficacy until we find ourselves exhausted and in professional exile—either by our own doing or with the help of our employer. Ineffectiveness in our work can ultimately be traced back to a misappropriation of our strengths.

Dr. Chip Anderson said it best: "A person's strengths employed in the wrong context ultimately beats them up." For example, if you are predisposed to function strategically yet find yourself in a job that is committed to doing things as they have always been done, you will likely be extremely frustrated, dissatisfied, and ripe for burnout. Your work will likely begin to falter.

In such situations, rather than address the "person-job-fit" issue or the way we do our job by considering our *Personal Owner's Manual*, we attempt to identify "weaknesses" in our performance and ways to compensate for them. Mihaly Csikszentmihalyi (2003) writes, "A job that employs only a fraction of one's skills quickly becomes a burden. One feels that most of one's potential is left unused, wasted.... When most of one's skills remain unengaged, involvement in the job soon falters, and it is not surprising that one begins to yearn for free time, where there is a chance to be fully alive" (p. 94).

It's How We Do the Job

Finding a job that draws upon our strengths pays big dividends in the internal rewards department. Sadly, the large majority of Americans indicate that they are moderately to greatly dissatisfied with their jobs. Two factors may significantly contribute to this malaise. One is the person-job-fit issue. Another is a need to reframe how we execute our day-to-day activities; sometimes, jobs can be tolerated or even enjoyed when the fit is not ideal if we find ways to draw on our Design to accomplish the work.

Engagement on the job drastically increases when workers feel that their strengths are employed on a consistent basis. Managers often fail to consider the remarkable relationship between the quality of employee performance and engagement on the job. Conversely, an individual can take a position that seems to have all of the qualities that matter most to them—even one that appears compatible with their "proficiencies" or strengths—but the organizational culture might make it a poor match. Yet most job decisions are based on proficiencies alone.

Leaders, managers, and human resources personnel should work with employees to develop a personalized plan for executing their job responsibilities. The more employees feel a sense of ownership in their work, the more likely they are to be happy and willing to stay with the organization.

Person-Job-Fit Matters

Many years ago, a Chief Operating Officer (COO) of a medium-size corporation approached my former consulting firm with a request for executive coaching and an organizational health appraisal. The gentleman had become acquainted with our services after attending a workshop we facilitated at a national conference and watching some of our online videos. He recognized that although he was at the pinnacle of his career in terms of position and compensation, he had several "rough areas" that he wanted to address through leadership coaching as he concurrently worked on improving his organization.

Our consulting firm was excited to engage this client. We knew that combining professional (personal) and organizational (company) development can result in a comprehensive transformational process. This executive was an exceptional employee who had worked his way up the corporate ladder primarily within his current company. He was so committed to its success that after attending our seminar, he recognized that it would benefit everyone if he better understood how to develop and channel his strengths while also learning how to mitigate some of his liabilities.

The client's corporation had been in existence for more than fifty years and boasted a multigenerational workforce and clientele. Despite its long-term success, the company was beginning to falter due to an increasingly competitive marketplace attributed in part to the advent of the internet. The company saw decreased profits while operational costs skyrocketed.

We introduced the client to a series of activities to help him understand his Design and apply this knowledge in his personal and professional life. He became excited about his growth, and would regularly share his experiences with his wife and teenage daughter. His daughter was so intrigued with his "homework" that while he developed his own *Personal Owner's Manual*, she developed hers.

People at work noticed a change in our client. He exuded greater confidence in his decision making. He was more sensitive in situations that previously would have made him erupt with rage, then follow up with apologies. He reorganized his workday around activities that maximized his *flow* (more on this later). The more he approached his profession with intentionality, the more adept he became at creatively addressing problem areas of the corporation. Divisions that had faced losses for several quarters were becoming profitable again. He was ecstatic. Long-term employees who had been largely apathetic and even a little cynical were suddenly becoming excited about their work and offering suggestions.

Not everyone, however, was pleased with what was happening. Despite the fact that everything our client was doing was within the purview of his job description as COO, and the fact that his actions ultimately benefited everyone, the CEO resisted. At first, this resistance manifested as silence. Then he expressed his malcontent by altering his relationship with his second in command. A years-long partnership grounded in friendship become increasingly awkward. Casual conversations between the two executives ceased, and the CEO reversed his longstanding open-door policy.

Confused, the COO scrutinized his actions and the recent devolution of his relationship with his boss. He decided to broach the subject with the CEO during a twice-rescheduled, one-on-one meeting. As was his custom, the COO discussed the past month's performance, highlighting challenges and the strategies he had used to address them. He emphasized how the actions helped increase profitability. He became visibly moved when he discussed how employees who for years had focused only on their impending retirement, doing no more than what was required, were now staying longer to complete tasks and offering up suggestions during team meetings.

The CEO stared at him, his face reddening. The CEO then stated emphatically that all improvement strategies in process were to cease. Any future changes would be facilitated by the office of the CEO.

Feeling deflated, the COO left the meeting and went offsite to ponder the exchange. He cared deeply for his boss. He wanted so badly for the organization to succeed. He was thrilled that employees were suddenly excited about coming to work and contributing to the change process. They knew the corporation had been on a downward spiral, and now they felt ownership for its future. Their actions could potentially alter its trajectory.

As the COO pondered the situation, one thing became clear: While he could discontinue the change efforts within the organization, he could not undo what he had learned about himself. The time spent exploring his Design, crafting a *Personal Owner's Manual*, and using his newfound self-knowledge to personalize his life and his work could not be undone. He was different. He saw his world through a sharper lens. Inherent within his Design was the capacity and corresponding passion to positively impact organizations. He faced the sobering reality that this was not the right fit for him, and that he needed to make a change.

Besides, it was inevitable that without a revolutionary series of changes, the corporation would soon cease to exist. It was clear that the CEO's ego would not entertain outside support, even if it cost the livelihood of hundreds of employees and their families. The CEO was incapable of assessing organizational vulnerabilities, crafting the right interventions, and rallying a team to execute the plan. He would go down with the ship, clinging to his nameplate designating him as CEO.

The COO could have felt defeated as he left the company. After all, he had invested nearly his entire professional career in the place. However, he walked away with a smile on his face, filled with optimism, and confident that he could apply what he had learned to make a difference elsewhere.

Toward Optimal Functioning: Flow

Leading by Design requires us to view our *Personal Owner's Manual* as a valuable resource to guide our choices and actions. Intentionality is the overarching virtue that helps us to realize a life well-lived.

Renowned psychologist Mihaly Csikszentmihalyi has invested his entire professional career in the science of optimal functioning. It is his belief that inherent within all people are ideal states that, if recognized and strategically replicated, can enable a person to flourish. This ideal state is often described as being "in the zone." It is a state of pure authenticity during which, whatever activity is being engaged, the person feels most natural or alive. Csikszentmihalyi (2003) calls this phenomena *flow*. He explains,

> The climber feels at one with the rock, the wind, and the weather; the musicians feel that the sounds they produce link them with the "harmony of the spheres"; the surgeon becomes part of the choreography of the operating theater; the dancer gets lost in the dance. After an episode of *flow* there is a sense that we have moved beyond our limitations, and have actually become a part of some great force, a system or process larger and more powerful than the individual selves we were before. (p. 390)

According to Csikszentmihalyi, his study of *flow* was prompted by a desire to study individuals who appeared to choose what they were doing with their lives and found enjoyment in the process. People who did what they did without the pressure of external rewards became the object of research for Csikszentmihalyi. In the mid-1970s, artists, rock climbers, musicians, and chess players, amongst others, provided valuable information. A universal sense of enjoyment of a particular activity produced such a state of euphoria that the subject would engage in that activity again and again. The reward was the activity itself.

Csikszentmihalyi (2000) called this state *flow* because "people describe their thoughts and actions when they are in the context as spontaneous and effortless, even though what they are doing is often difficult and risky. But at the time it feels as natural as being carried by the *flow* of a river, a process which does not require effort or control" (p. 389).

There are several commonly reported experiences shared by those claiming to access *flow* states. First, clear goals are evident every step of the way. The near-unconscious notes played by a musical performer best describe this characteristic. Csikszentmihalyi (1996) says, "When a job is enjoyable, it also has clear goals: The surgeon is aware how the incision should proceed moment by moment; the farmer has a plan for how to carry out the planting (p. 111)." Next, there is immediate feedback to one's actions. The individual knows the precise status of the activity. A keen ability to quickly assess the nature of the situation or activity is found in those who experience *flow*. Third, there is a balance between challenges and skill. The task is neither too easy nor too hard, but will always be challenging.

Next, action and awareness are merged—the person gets so involved in the chess game, or the climb, or the music, that action follows, seemingly without the intervention of a conscious self. A corollary effect of this deep concentration is that we tend to forget the worries and concerns that take up our attention in ordinary life. All of one's mental resources are taken up by the task at hand. In fact, all critical self-reflection disappears during the *flow* state, particularly as it relates to the assessment of others. The satisfaction enjoyed through the *flow* experience evaporates negative emotions.

Additionally, evidence demonstrates that the perpetuation of *flow* helps curb negative behaviors in children and adults. In his adaptation of *flow* theory into the corporate environment, Csikszentmihalyi (2003) writes, "Our research shows that teenagers who are in *flow* more often develop more productive habits: Not only are they much happier and more optimistic, and have higher self-esteem, but they study more, are involved in active leisure more often, and spend more time with friends—a finding that is independent of income, parental education, and social status. Adults who are more often in *flow* are not only happier, but they spend significantly more time at work actually working instead of gossiping, reading papers, or surfing the Web" (p. 69).

Think about an activity that make you feel truly yourself. It's unlikely that the positive effects experienced while engaging in that task is merely coincidental. Identifying catalysts for optimal functioning provides a window onto the masterpiece of your identity. Ask yourself: *What activities cause you to feel most alive? What are you doing when you lose all sense of time? How can you incorporate flow-inducing activities into your life on a more regular basis?*

The questions posed above are things you'll consider in the fourth and final chapter of this book. While the first three chapters provided stories, examples, and suggestions to set you on a path of self-discovery, Chapter Four will guide you through the process of discovering your Design and creating your own *Personal Owner's Manual.* I think you'll enjoy the process, and I sincerely hope you're excited to get started!

Notes

Record memories, insights, and epiphanies here
so that you can refer to them later.

Notes

Notes

Notes

Chapter Four: Deciphering Your Design—
The Personal Owner's Manual

"Although we may at times be blessed naturally with a state of inner clarity and quiet, the only reliable method of reaching it comes through our intent, making a conscious choice to step back from the work and our urgent concerns. Listening, waiting, ripening, and embracing 'not-doing' engenders a fuller realization of our work at this stage. Returning to the banks of the river, moving out of the direct current, and resting or lying in the sun is not an idle activity. It is a highly necessary means of incubation, of reflection, of allowing the process to find its own shape and momentum, and of finding room for the unexpected insight and the on-the-edge-of-consciousness discovery." David Ulrich

"What can we gain by sailing to the moon if we are not able to cross the abyss that separates us from ourselves? This is the most important of all voyages of discovery, and without it all the rest are not only useless but disastrous." Thomas Merton

"Allow your judgements their own silent, undisturbed development, which like all progress, must come from deep within and cannot be forced or hastened. Everything is gestation and then birthing. To let each impression and each embryo of a feeling come to completion, entirely in itself, in the dark, in the unsayable, the unconscious, beyond the reach of one's own understanding, and with deep humility and patience to wait for the hour when a new clarity is born: this alone is what it means to live as an artist: in understanding as in creating. In this there is no measuring with time, a year doesn't

matter, and ten years are nothing. Being an artist means: not numbering and counting, but ripening like a tree, which doesn't force its sap, and stands confidently in the storms of spring, not afraid that afterward summer may not come. It does come. But it comes only to those who are patient…. I learn it every day of my life, learn it with pain I am grateful for: patience is everything!" Rilke

Learning, living, and leading by Design ensures that our life makes an indelible impression upon the world. It requires a willingness to engage in introspection, integration, and intervention. Introspection helps us discover our *birthright gifts* and discern our Design. Integration brings the various dimensions of the self into alignment with one's Design. A life of purpose is one that's dedicated to intervention, to making a positive difference.

When we're living a life of purpose, we seek opportunities to utilize our Design through our work, relationships, and interactions with others in our communities. In the process, we engage in *flow*-inducing activities, which promise personal satisfaction, happiness, creativity, and commitment. What wonderful gifts we can give ourselves—and others—when we pay attention to our Design!

The remainder of this book takes you through a process for discovering your Design and developing a *Personal Owner's Manual* that will help you learn, live, and lead by Design.

The Personal Owner's Manual Retreat

"We do not go into the desert to escape people but to learn how to find them; we do not leave them in order to have nothing more to do with them, but to find out the way to do them the most good. But this is only the secondary end." Thomas Merton

"Often we want to be somewhere other than where we are, to even be someone other than who we are. We tend to compare ourselves constantly with others and wonder why we are not as rich, as intelligent, as simple, as generous, or as saintly as they are. Such comparisons make us feel guilty, ashamed, or jealous. It is very important to realize that our vocation is hidden in where we are and who we are. We are unique human beings, each with a call to realize in life what nobody else can, and to realize it in the concrete context of the here and now. We will never find our vocations by trying to figure out whether we are better or worse than others. We are good enough to do what we are called to do. Be yourself!" Henri J. Nouwen

Few of us have the luxury of being able to retreat totally from our busy lives for days at time in order to contemplate the mysteries of our unique Design or to create a *Personal Owner's Manual.* The multitude of voices and responsibilities competing for our attention can be deafening. The ringing cell phone, the intrusive meeting notification, the vibrating smartwatch telling us to get up and burn more calories—these and other distractions will almost surely interrupt our efforts.

No worries! You can build a series of "mini-retreats" into your regular schedule over a period of several days or weeks. Taking the time for a thoughtful approach over time has some advantages over attempting to complete the manual in a day or two. Here are a few suggestions for planning your retreat (or mini-retreats):

- **Timing:** Schedule time for development of your *Personal Owner's Manual* just as you would an important meeting. Think about your typical day. Choose a time when you feel most creative and alert.

- **Place:** Find or create an inviting place. It should be comfortable, safe, and inspiring.

- **Format:** You may wish to transfer each section of your *Personal Owner's Manual* to a notebook since you will likely need more writing space than this book provides. Later, you may want to create a visually appealing, cleaned-up version in a word processing program.

- **Noise:** Consider briefly fasting from technology. Constant calls, alerts, notifications, and reminders disrupt our thoughts, clutter our minds, and distract us from the important creative task at hand.

- **Journaling**: In addition to developing your *Personal Owner's Manual*, have a journal nearby in which you can document a "history" of your experience. When something comes to mind, write it down, regardless of whether it makes sense at the time. Sometimes our minds reveal important details or thoughts that can help us understand the "bigger picture" later on. Also, journaling helps us transfer our dilemmas, difficult memories, or important decisions from our psyche to paper. The act of getting "stuff" out of our heads and placing it someplace else can be extremely therapeutic and can help us think about those things with greater objectivity.

- **Motion:** To help stimulate your creativity, take a walk or go for a jog. Sometimes breakthroughs occur as we engage in movement. Movement can be especially helpful before you begin reflecting and writing for the day, or when you need a break.

- **Focus**: The task of developing a comprehensive *Personal Owner's Manual* may seem daunting. It is an attempt to capture the totality of one's known and unknown constitution and to make sense of it. Rather than tackling the entire project at once, devote your attention to only one section at a time. Eventually, you will identify important linkages and relationships.

- **Analogies**: Devote part of your retreat to spending time outdoors. There are many important messages communicated to us all the time. Most go unheard, though, because we are not listening or watching. What might a starry sky, a colony of ants hard at work, or a mountain peak peering out of the clouds be saying to you today?

- **Growth:** Commit to seeking out continual opportunities to explore and reinforce your Design. Creating your *Personal Owner's Manual* is a great place to start. Once you've done that, you will probably find yourself gravitating toward books and conversations with others that further raise your level of consciousness. As your thoughts, feelings, fears, joys, defeats, and victories intersect with those of others, their stories become part of yours. You will see not only the trees, but a lush forest.

- **Commitment**: Identify one or two people with whom you are comfortable sharing all aspects of your journey. Seeking feedback from people you trust, who know you well, can provide valuable insights and perspectives. Share your goals for completing your *Personal Owner's Manual* with them. Ask them to hold you accountable to see it through its completion. The shared journey will provide both of you with a valuable gift. Better yet, they may be inspired to work on their own *Personal Owner's Manual* while you do yours. What a wonderful opportunity for a distinct, yet shared, experience of self-discovery and planning!

• **Goal Setting:** Virtually every component of your *Personal Owner's Manual* challenges you to take action. Consider creating short- and long-term goals in each of the five key areas (Overview, Distinguishing Features, Requirements for Optimal Functioning, Precautions, and Support). Make sure your short-term goals or "small victories" are realistic for you. Identify benchmarks to help you determine how and when you have made progress. For long-term goals, think about the big picture. What does your preferred future look like? How will you know you have "arrived"?

Step-by-step guidance for creating your manual starts on the next page.

Developing Your Personal Owner's Manual

Section One: Overview: Who I am and Why I am Here

IMPORTANT: Read the instructions and questions in this section, but don't work on Section One of your *Personal Owner's Manual* until after you have completed sections Two through Five. Those sections will guide you through a process for discovering your Design. During that process, you will generate a great deal of information about yourself. Recording this information will enable you to identify meaningful patterns that tell a very personal story. Only then will you be prepared to address the questions below, which pertain to purpose.

A. Statement of Purpose

Before you complete the statements below, respond to the "tough questions" in Part B of this section.

Complete the following statement. Be as specific as possible:

Based upon thoughtful consideration of my Design as I completed Sections Two through Five of my *Personal Owner's Manual, as well as the questions in Part B of Section One,* this is what I believe about my purpose in this life (why I'm here at this time and place):

_____

_____

_____

_____

_____

Design

Complete the following statement based on epiphanies you had while reading this book and completing your *Personal Owner's Manual:*

The most significant evidence of my purpose is

_____

_____

_____

_____

_____

B. The Tough Questions

***Respond to the following questions after you have completed Section Five of your Personal Owner's Manual. ***

1. From where do you find meaning and purpose in your life?

2. What two or three things do you love most about yourself?

3. Are you overly consumed with your imperfections? Does your preoccupation with "what is wrong" cause you to overlook what is right and good about your Design? How might you adjust your focus?

4. When you contemplate your work, does it feel like a job, a career, or a calling? Explain. If you would like to shift the way you regard your work, would you want it to feel like a job, a career, or a calling? What current factors make the desired change difficult? What are some *untried* strategies you can employ to make the change a reality?

5. Historically, do you believe you have had any influence over the course of your life, or has life just "happened"?

6. Living with intentionality does not mean that adverse circumstances will not happen to us. They are inevitable. However, if you don't feel like you have much control over the big stuff, what are some small areas in your life in which you DO have control? Based on what you know about yourself, where might you exert greater control?

7. When you consider your Design, what can *you* do to perpetuate the evolution of humankind? What *new* things can you do to make a positive difference in the lives of others? Describe ways you can utilize your Design to better your . . .

Personal Life:

Professional Life:

Section Two: Distinguishing Features

This section of your Personal Owner's Manual includes three parts: (A) Recovering Wonder, (B) Birthright Gifts Analysis, and (C) Identity Matrix. Each part includes questions that prompt you to think deeply about past and present thoughts and feelings. Take your time. It may be helpful to reread Chapter One as you complete this section. You may also wish to consult the glossary to review the meaning of important words or concepts.

A. Recovering Wonder: Remember Life Before *The Nothing* and Looking Ahead

Earliest Recollections	The Attack	Right Now	Remaining Young
What provoked wonder in you as a child? What are your earliest memories of being in awe?	When and how did *The Nothing* first attempt to diminish your sense of wonder? Were *The Nothing's* efforts successful? Explain what happened. At the time, were you aware of *The Nothing*?	What fills you with wonder now? How often do you experience this?	What steps can you take to cultivate and retain a "fresh young mind"? Be specific. What can you do to continue learning, right now and in the future, regardless of your age?

B. *Birthright Gifts* Analysis

Birthright gifts are clues to our identity and calling that often emerge at a very early stage in our lives. They may be triggered by childhood experiences that seem mysterious yet positive, making us want to repeat the experience and the feelings they evoke. The prompts below will help you identify three of your *birthright gifts* by considering early behaviors and reactions. As you explore the various ways these gifts showed themselves, watch for themes or patterns. Feel free to reference the author's analysis of his own gifts in Chapter Two. You may also wish to see the glossary for a more detailed explanation of *birthright gifts*, Dreamstealers, and Dreamstarters. Identifying *birthright gifts* requires going back in time to recall early memories. The exercise below will help.

Exercise B-1: Creative Prethinking: Below are some questions to help you get started in the identification of your *birthright gifts*. Take some time for brainstorming and thoughtful reflection, and jot down your responses. Then take a few steps back to see if certain themes (gifts) emerge. Once you have identified three of your birthright gifts, use Exercise B-2 to explore each gift in greater depth.

As a child . . .

- Were there certain activities to which you frequently gravitated? Explain your attraction to them. What made you keep returning to those activities?

- Did certain things come especially easy to you? What were they? How did you know you had an "edge"?

- What made you feel most alive?

- What did you like most about yourself?

- Was anything that you were especially good at the source of ridicule (from peers, family, or others)?

- What was the object of your playtime? On what did you focus? What were you doing? Were any of your "playtime" behaviors also present in other situations?

- Were you formally or informally recognized for any behaviors or skills as a child? What were they? How did the recognition make you feel?

- Did you have any recurring positive dreams (or daydreams) in which you were the star? What were you doing? How did you feel upon waking?

If after this brainstorming session you feel like you still do not have an idea of what your *birthright gifts* might be, consider sharing the above questions with someone who knew you well as a child, and asking for their input.

Exercise B-2: Birthright Gifts Profile

GIFT #1: _____

Clues	Response	Development	To Do
How did the gift first emerge? What were you doing? Who noticed it?	How was the gift nurtured? Did a *Dreamstarter* respond to this gift? Describe the encounter. Did a Dreamstealer attempt to discredit this gift? What happened?	Has the gift developed and evolved into current usage? If so, how? Is the gift now dormant or unused? Did its evolution stop for some reason? Why?	What steps can you take to further develop and apply this *birthright gift*? If you were influenced by one or more Dreamstealers, what steps can you take to diminish the damage and move forward? Who can now serve as a *Dreamstarter*?

GIFT #2: _____

Clues	Response	Development	To Do
How did the gift first emerge? What were you doing? Who noticed it?	How was the gift nurtured? Did a *Dreamstarter* respond to this gift? Describe the encounter. Did a Dreamstealer attempt to discredit this gift? What happened?	Has the gift developed and evolved into current usage? If so, how? Is the gift now dormant or unused? Did its evolution stop for some reason? Why?	What steps can you take to further develop and apply this *birthright gift*? If you were influenced by one or more Dreamstealers, what steps can you take to diminish the damage and move forward? Who can now serve as a *Dreamstarter*?

Design

GIFT #3: _____

Clues	Response	Development	To Do
How did the gift first emerge? What were you doing? Who noticed it?	How was the gift nurtured? Did a *Dreamstarter* respond to this gift? Describe the encounter. Did a Dreamstealer attempt to discredit this gift? What happened?	Has the gift developed and evolved into current usage? If so, how? Is the gift now dormant or unused? Did its evolution stop for some reason? Why?	What steps can you take to further develop and apply this *birthright gift*? If you were influenced by one or more Dreamstealers, what steps can you take to diminish the damage and move forward? Who can now serve as a *Dreamstarter*?

C. Identity Matrix

The questions below prompt you to consider three important areas—your passions, your proficiencies, and your personality. As you respond to these prompts, look for any patterns that emerge. What do those patterns say about your Design? How can you develop and channel these assets into your personal life? Your work?

Passions

What positive things do you dream about?

What gets you excited?

How do you currently engage those passions?

Identify strategies that could be developed to allow for greater engagement or realization of your passions. Explain.

Proficiencies

In what areas do you excel (personal or professional)?

What are your strengths? (Be specific.)

How can you nurture your strengths?

What threats exist to the development of your strengths, and how can you mitigate those threats?

Identify ways in which you can strategically apply your strengths in areas in which you want to excel.

Personality

What makes your personality unique?

Have you completed personality assessments before? Are there certain consistencies between the results? What do they say about you?

Are there certain aspects of your personality that you keep repressed? Why? What advantages might there be in revealing more about your unique identity to others? What dangers might there be?

Section Three: Requirements for Optimal Functioning

Think about what you need in order to be at your best.

A. Creative Disruption Exercise

Daily routines and habits may or may not contribute to our best self. Often, we do things a certain way simply because someone else told us to, or because we've always done it that way—not because it's the best or easiest or most natural way.

Have you ever examined your regular activities to determine whether they complement or act as an obstacle to your Design? Have you tried different routines or environments to see what works best for you?

Leadership coach David Ulrich (2002) says some of our most deeply engrained behaviors may, in fact, diminish our performance. He suggests that a disruption in routines can reveal a great deal about who we really are. "If you like to write in solitude, try writing in a noisy café," he suggests. "If you work best in the early morning, try working in the evening. Approach yourself as a question. What really helps you get to work? What conditions do you need, really, to pursue your aims with energy and vitality?" (p. 141).

Try this: Identify two or three of your daily behaviors or routines, and create an intentional disruption. Then reflect on the results: How did you react to the change? What did you learn about yourself? Did the new behavior or routine better correspond to your Design? Will you continue to follow the new routine, return to the old one, or try a different disruption? Record your findings in the space that follows.

> **Example:**
>
> **Routine/Behavior:** *Drive my car to work.*
>
> **Proposed Disruption:** *Take a bus to work.*
>
> **Observations (after trying the disruption):** *Felt stressed when bus was late. Took longer than usual to get to work. Tried to read on bus, but was unable to focus. This experiment made me more aware of time spent in transit (20 minutes each way = 3 hours and 20 minutes a week). How can I make better use of that time?*
>
> **Proposed Changes to Routine/Pattern:** *Continue to drive car to work, but listen to podcasts or audiobooks to make drive more interesting and productive.*

Routine/Behavior #1:

_____

_____

Proposed Disruption:

_____

_____

Observations (after trying the disruption):

_____

_____

_____

Proposed Changes to Routine/Pattern:

_____

_____

_____

_____

Routine/Behavior #2:

_____

_____

Proposed Disruption:

_____

_____

Observations (after trying the disruption):

_____

_____

_____

_____

Proposed Changes to Routine/Pattern:

_____

_____

_____

_____

Routine/Behavior #3:

_____

_____

Proposed Disruption:

_____

_____

Observations (after trying the disruption):

_____

_____

_____

_____

Proposed Changes to Routine/Pattern:

_____

_____

_____

_____

B. *Flow* Analysis

Think about activities that provide a "mountaintop experience" for you. The more regularly we do activities that cause this state of *flow*, the more likely we are to feel engaged, happy, creative, and purposeful.

Activity	Effects	Personal Response	Replication Strategies
What are you doing that causes you to be "in the zone"?	How do you know you are "in the zone"? (Be specific.) Some examples: 1. Distortion of time 2. Becoming one with the task or "losing oneself" 3. Heightened concentration 4. Balance of difficulty and likelihood of success	How does it make you feel?	How can you integrate *flow*-inducing activities more often into your daily routine?

Section Four: Precautions

Strategies for Preventing Harm

Use the prompts below to help you consider your liabilities—personal behaviors or tendencies that can result in undesirable consequences for yourself or others. What are these liabilities? How do they manifest themselves? What can be done to ensure that no one is harmed by them? How can you better contain them? Diminish them? Consider your life at home, at work, at school, and in social situations.

Liability: Identify an undesirable behavior that can potentially inflict harm upon others. If nothing comes to mind, consider asking someone who knows you well and will be forthright. Describe.

_____

_____

_____

_____

_____

_____

Origin: Can you identify the root/cause/origin of this liability (bad behavior)? Was it incurred as a result of a Dreamstealer? If so, explain.

_____

_____

_____

_____

_____

_____

Triggers: What events or circumstances promulgate this "bad behavior"? In other words, what sets you off?

_____

_____

_____

_____

_____

_____

Strategies: What steps can you take to address your liabilities? Could the likelihood of inflicting harm on others be decreased by forgiving a person who may have hurt you along the way? Do you need someone to help you work through this process? Consider developing a plan of action with short- and long-term goals. How will you respond to your triggers in a more constructive/ positive way?

_____

_____

_____

_____

_____

_____

Section Five: Support

Reflection and Planning

Reflect on each of the questions below, and record your ideas. Your responses will help you plan ahead so that you can respond effectively to challenges as they arise.

- To whom can you turn when you are not functioning optimally (at your best)?

- How will this person know that you need support?

- Who knows you well enough to reinforce your Design and honor your commitment to living according to your *Personal Owner's Manual?*

- Who will be honest with you, even when the information may not be what you want to hear?

- Who do you know who has similar Design specifications that can help you with your development?

- Who can serve as a role model or mentor? How can you approach this person to see if he or she is willing to work with you?

- With whom can you share your *Personal Owner's Manual?* Some people enjoy discussing their journey with a friend or loved one. Sharing your manual can lead to meaningful conversations, insights, and affirmations. It's also a way to hold oneself accountable for making progress on action items.

Reminder: Now that you have completed Sections Two through Five of your *Personal Owner's Manual,* go back to Section One, respond to the questions presented in Part B of that section, and write your statement of purpose in Part A.

You Did It! Now What?

Congratulations! You have completed a creative process of remembering, recording, discovering, envisioning, and planning that will forever change the way you think about yourself, your purpose, and what's possible. I'm confident that the discoveries you made will empower you to live a more productive and fulfilling life, to continue learning and growing, and to lead others in contributing to worthwhile endeavors.

But the journey's not over. It has just begun! Here's one simple thing you can do to keep yourself moving forward:

Right now, pull out your calendar and schedule an hour or two every quarter for the next year to review your *Personal Owner's Manual,* record any new insights into your Design, and renew your commitment to living by Design.

You're also invited to visit my website for additional ideas and inspiration. I'd love to hear about your discoveries and how you're putting them to use!

You may reach me at anthonyjmarchese.com.

Notes

Notes

Notes

Appendix A: Full Transcript of Author's Conversation with Kameel Srouji

The book that I'm currently working on is based on the idea that God's creative fingerprints are all over every human being and when we identify and develop those, it moves us toward understanding our calling—why we're on this planet—because I don't believe we're here by accident.

I am with you one hundred percent because I believe that. My sister, Aviva, said, "God wanted you to come to America to make a difference with food, to change lives."

This makes me think of a couple of my regular customers. One of them is an attorney. When we met four years ago when we first opened, he weighed 325 pounds. He eats with us at least four times a week when he is not traveling. He has lost 50 pounds since he started dining with us. Another gentleman who was there when you were there lost 25 pounds in six months. He said, "Kameel, my doctor is amazed." A lady who was suffering from diabetes came by one of my restaurants by accident and she ate with me right before she went to the doctor for a checkup. He said, "Ma'am I don't know what you just had or what you did yesterday or this morning, but keep doing it. She said, "I just went to this Mediterranean restaurant. He said, "I want you to go there again."

So the effects were immediate? That's amazing.

Immediate. Because the product that we were serving her was one hundred percent organic turkey and vegetables. I only use olive oil. I do not add butter. I do not add any artificial flavoring into my food.

Is it unusual for a Mediterranean restaurant to serve food free of additives or butter?

This is the difference between my food and other similar restaurants. It goes back to calling. In the other places, instead of lemon juice, they use citric acid. They make things like tabbouleh. They make tahini. They may use a little lemon juice but it's mostly citric acid to give it an intense lemon flavor. In America, you can buy garlic spread. It is delicious. Guess what? It's full of citric acid. People in America don't take an extra few minutes of their time to ask what is in the food.

I recently went to a popular fast food restaurant and asked the manager, "How often do you change your oil in the fryer?" The guy, who was a very smart guy, said, "When it starts turning brown."

When I fry my falafel, I use olive oil only. I only fry with it once. I do not reuse my oil. I believe we may be the only place in the world that fries falafel in olive oil. Guess what? It costs me more money, but I want people to be so healthy that they say, "I want to go to Aviva again and again. I feel better about myself." This is my philosophy: If I don't eat it, my customers will never eat it. That is what I teach my employees.

And some of my employees end up leaving my business to seek another opportunity. Guess what? Ninety percent will come back. "Kameel, you put something in your food that is very addictive and we have to come back and work for you." It gives me the chills when an employee comes back and says, "I want to work for you again." Because they realize when they go out there that it's not the same. And one of the reasons is I do not open for dinner. I wish you'd come by in about two hours. We scrub the whole restaurant, from the bathroom to the kitchen, with bleach and scouring powder—the floors and all of the equipment. We do not do it twice a week. We do it every night. We strip the whole place down.

It was very clean.

Even if you go to our bathrooms, it's the same thing. We strip it down. My walk-in cooler is also the same. You know, I also go to the market for fresh produce two to three times a week. This also helps keep everything clean.

I'm enjoying this baklava.

You're talking about this Middle Eastern food? [Points to baklava.] This here? Most baklava is saturated with butter. Clarified butter. You have to make it clarified. I don't because of my mom. She used to make her pastries with olive oil.

That's got olive oil in it?

Olive oil.

That's some of the best baklava I've ever had.

It does actually. For me it is the best. When you eat baklava, because of the fat, it's going to stay on the roof of your mouth and stick to your tongue. This goes down fast with nothing but a sip of water.

145

So it's unusual to make it with olive oil.

Oh, nobody makes it like this.

Is this something you decided to do?

Yes, because I watched my mom. She used to make Danishes but with one hundred percent olive oil.

So with this baklava, I use one hundred percent organic maple syrup. We get six, fifty-pound tubs from Vermont, and we pay between $250 and $300 per tub. It will cost me almost double the amount than if I were to buy sugar or regular butter.

So what people do not understand is that there is a product on the market that is very similar to butter. It is similar to butter in taste. It has the same flavor. It is chemically manufactured. If you want to eat something that tastes like butter, go eat butter. Alternatives are so horrible for you. Those Middle Eastern restaurants use that alternative product instead of butter so that they can make it cheap. And it sells. Also, you know what else? There is no honey in baklava.

Really?

I'm telling you. There's no honey in there. What they often use is one hundred percent white sugar. The Greeks? Most of them, they use corn syrup, and they add some spices to it and thin it down a little bit and they call it honey. The consumer is always in a hurry. "Give me something I can eat in my car while I'm driving. Give me that fast food sandwich. Give me those eggs." Some of the fast food places are starting to use real eggs. This is good because most always used egg powder. You have to add a

146

million items to the powder to keep it fresh. Lots of preservatives. At Aviva, that is not something that we do.

Interesting. When you think about why you're here— and I'm not talking about just in Atlanta—why are you on this planet? What is your calling?

God brought me to America to spread the words from the Old Testament. Give them the best because God, He loves the best. He always wanted the best. He said it many times. "I'm the only God and you respect me." And that's why I was always fascinated with Abraham and how he went out of his way...look, Isaac. Abraham. He took the biggest sheep God gave him. He did not go and get it. God brought it for him, right? He could have brought him a pig or he could have brought him anything. A sheep. Clean. Beautiful. And Jesus become the lamb of God. There's a relationship to me.

When you say to a customer, and maybe it's a stranger, or maybe it's their first time, when you say "I love you," what do you mean?

A long time ago when different countries had kings, when you saw the king, what did you do? You took his hand. You kissed it. It is similar today, when you see the Pope. The most amazing thing for me is my dream to touch the Pope's hand and to kiss his ring. When I think of the Pope: "Listen, you are the man of God. I just want to touch you." Look at the lady in the New Testament. All she wanted to do was just touch Jesus's robe and she was healed. He said, "Your faith...." You know what I'm talking about. It gives me goosebumps. And when my customers come in [I tell them] "I love you for not only coming in to eat my food but for supporting me. You allow me to help make lives better. What could be better than this? You're giving me life to keep going, to breathe, to spend my energy making the best food there is. Within my mind and heart is a desire to give the best, so of course I'm going to love you."

One of the things when I left your restaurant, I was just thinking about all of the bad stuff that is going on in the world—wars, terrorism, terrible things. I think about our technology. We are constantly getting pushed information through electronic notifications of all of these negative things. During my visit to Aviva, very few people were staring at their phones. What do you think about that, and does your restaurant play a part in offering customers a reprieve from so much negativity?

I tell my customers, "Guys, we need to love one another." When you turn around at the church, you shake your neighbor's hand, right? What do you tell them?

Peace, peace be with you.

I tell my customers the same thing. When you pass the falafel plate while you are waiting to order in the line, tell others that you love them. Because what's happening around the world is all about money and power. It is so sad. People have lost the feeling that God has brought us here for a reason. We're killing each other. I tell them to tell others that you love them because we need love.

When you think about your life, what ultimate legacy do you want to leave?

I want people to say, "This man, he showed us the right way to nourish our bodies." That's all. I'm not thinking about money.

I'm not thinking about anything but for people to say, "He made a difference in my life in how I eat and how I'm going to feed my family."

I also want to be known for helping others.

Let me give you an example. A couple of days ago we had a huge party at lunch time.

Their bill was $3,500.

The party that we were to serve consisted of one hundred and ten people who worked for a company around here. The company does a quarterly employee lunch and treats their people nicely. They go all the way. We sent our staff to wait for them and clean up afterwards. We had some leftover beef tenderloin at the restaurant and I thought I would treat my employees because of all their hard work. You know what chateaubriand is, right? So we took the filet from on top. I realized that though I could make an additional $400 by selling the leftovers as kababs, I thought, many of these employees cannot afford filet mignon at their home." I offered it to them. You should have seen their faces. It made me happy to hear them say, "I get to eat black angus filet!" What could be better than to see somebody that is happy to have a chance to try this quality of beef?

Yesterday was the first day off I've had in about two months. I always work on Saturdays and Sundays. My son was concerned. He said, "Your life...." My attorney said, "Kameel, don't you want to go visit someplace?" I said, "Yeah. I want to take a vacation." But guess what? I'm happy. I love what I do. You know, for you to go to Vegas or to go to Florida is a big deal. For me, to see somebody healthy, somebody shedding some weight off, this is my vacation. Yeah. You say, "That cannot be. That's not normal." I said, "It is for me. I'm content. I'm happy. If I could put eight days in a week, I'd put eight days in."

You seem content with your life.

If you asked me today, "Would you change your life?" I would say no. I'm here for a reason. I'm not going to die until that reason gets accomplished. I feel my purpose coming alive through all of the support that I receive from my customers. Listen. How many places do you really see that have customers who travel and then bring you back special items? I get so many cigars, which I enjoy once every two months or so. I sit outside on my balcony and I build a fire and I smoke one and enjoy it. They also bring me olive oil. They bring me wine. One person came about two weeks ago and had been in Rome. He went to the Cathedral and he brought me back some small icons. Here in Atlanta, we had a priest convention and there were orthodox priests from all over the world—from Russia and other places. You know, I get letters sent to me from Rome that say God sent you here for a mission. I swear. I will show you.

I believe you. And that's why I'm here talking to you, because after I was at your restaurant I felt like I had been someplace special. You know when you go to church and you worship God and you sing and you pray and you hear a homily or a sermon, you know how you feel? That's how I felt coming to your restaurant, and I needed to know your story, and I want to tell your story.

Look at what the priest gave me. His words touched my heart. He said, "God brought you here for a reason and you're showing it to your customers. That's the true Jesus in you." I mean, he gave me the goosebumps and he sent me a letter. With that it said keep doing it because that's what God brought you to this world for. God is good.

He is.

So I'm going to continue in my path every single day and I want to get better every single day. I want to make sure my consumers are getting better every day.

You know so much about food. I noticed that you like to educate your customers.

Some might say we are not making enough profit on our items. But I say, look at the volume. For example, farm-raised salmon sells at local restaurants for $27 to $32. We sell organic salmon for $14 and you get two sides with it.

We only eat at a couple of places here in Atlanta because I know they're really clean—a piece of salmon by itself with a little bit of kale mixed in is $27.95 and it's not even organic. It's just a regular piece of salmon. And people do not understand when I tell them I refuse to serve anything farm-raised. I refuse to buy chicken dipped in a chlorine bath because people do not understand that maybe about eighty percent of chicken here in America is put in a chlorine bath. The regular chicken—not kosher, not organic— the not-natural way they put it in a chlorine bath to give it whiter color and to kill salmonella. Go back to the news story where Germany refused a whole shipment of chicken from the U.S. It happened about six months or a year ago. They refused the whole shipment and they brought it back to America when they found out it was dipped in chlorine.

Back here in Georgia, I had someone apply to work with me who was from Panama. Unfortunately, she didn't have any papers with her. She was working with an American chicken manufacturer and some of that solution, even though they make them wear gloves up to here, somehow some of that bleach solution seeped through and her arm was burned. It's a big pool of chlorine. If you look at the color of chicken it is very white. That's the reason why. And then we eat it. I mean, think about the chicken that we eat in America. How old do you think that every piece of chicken that you buy from the supermarket is? At least four or five weeks old.

Weeks? Wow.

Here's the reason. They slaughter it and they put in there and they put it in a freezing temperature and then it goes from the manufacturer to the broker, who ends up sending it to the supermarket. Transportation. All that counts too. Think about the time it takes for the stores to get it out of the freezer and then put it on the shelf to thaw out. So think about it. How long would it take from A to Z? Yes, there is some chicken that is only about one week old, like the organic chicken that you get at the store, and you pay about $6.99 to $9.99 per pound. It depends on which farm it came from and the diet they gave the chicken. But the organic products now? In the last eight years...wow. People are buying more and more. And here's the beautiful thing about America right now. People are changing. In the last four years, people are understanding more, thank God.

And thank God for places like Aviva that explain to people what they are eating.

I noticed that on your television screens you not only have photos of food items but that you are also trying to provide

important health-related information to your consumers. Tell me about this.

That's what we do. We even tell them how to order when they come in. We have a screen to make it easier for them and for us so that we can get them through the line as fast as we can. We don't like people waiting in line for a long time. Even though they do have to wait—guess what? They're happy. We pass the falafel. We pass baklava for them, and they get that watermelon. Give thanks to the Lord. Give thanks to your customers. God gives us the soul and the customers have given me the support to keep doing business. It's beautiful.

It is beautiful. I think that I was supposed to come here to dine in your restaurant and to meet you.

I'm so glad.

I really do. I really do, and I can't wait to tell your story.

Please.

You know, always—and I tell this to my kids—always stay humble. Being rich is not about money. If you have a clean heart, God always provides. Look at the birds. He gives them feathers and a place to stay warm. Why do you want to worry about tomorrow? Tomorrow will take care of itself. This is my focus on life. He put me here for a reason and I'm going to continue no matter what. I went through some tough times. I lost all my money. Tomorrow's a brighter day because I believe He's going to give me the way to go. And He has. I'm telling you sometimes my heart will be dancing when I go to sleep. And I'm a different kind of man. Some might say I am in the Twilight Zone. I just love that experience, and I try so hard to go into these deep thoughts because I just want to touch His robe one day. You know, I cannot wait, and I try so hard. He already gave me my path. I just want to touch His robe.

And I'm sure you will.

Well, thank you.

I really appreciate it.

And God bless you whatever you do.

Meeting you has been a gift.

Same here for me. Especially on Sunday. That's awesome.

Appendix B: Glossary

Birthright gifts: Our *birthright gifts* are natural gifts that often emerge very early in life and provide clues about our identity, calling, and Design. According to Parker Palmer, these gifts are subtle and can go unnoticed, but they often reveal themselves in unexpected ways as they vie for our attention. The more attentive we give to the way we respond to the world around us, the more our *birthright gifts* can help point us toward our authentic selves.

Calling: From the Latin, *vocatio*, a calling is similar to a purpose. Looking for patterns within our Design is a great way to better understand our calling. When we are engaged in activities related to our calling, we feel most alive.

Design: A person's Design consists of the collective passions, proficiencies, personality traits, and preferences that makes a person unique. *Birthright gifts* offer clues to a person's Design. Self-awareness of one's Design is the basis for creating a *Personal Owner's Manual*. No one ever has or ever will share your unique Design.

Dreamstarters: These are observant individuals who see our *birthright gifts* and point us toward our Design. They speak life into us by reminding us of who we really are. They encourage us to reach our full potential.

Dreamstealers: These are people who diminish others by emphasizing limitation over potential. Their words and actions may or may not be intentionally malicious, but regardless, they can invoke great harm and impede others' progress toward learning, living, and leading by Design.

Entelechies: This word, introduced by Aristotle, describes the internal drive that helps a living thing reach its full potential. For example, an acorn possesses entelechies that point it toward its potential of becoming an oak tree.

Flow: The concept of *flow*, popularized by Mihaly Csikszentmihalyi, says we are at our best when we are "in the zone." When we enter a flow state, we become completely immersed in the task at hand.

Personal Owner's Manual: This is a highly customized, comprehensive guide that reflects all the intricacies of one's Design. Development of a *Personal Owner's Manual* is a facilitated attempt to decipher one's own Design—and to identify strategies for increasing the level of personal investment in all one does in life.

Bibliography

Andersen, Hans Christian. 1837. *The Emperor's New Clothes*. J. Hersholt, trans. Retrieved from http://www.andersen.sdu.dk/vaerk/hersholt/TheEmperorsNewClothes_e.html.

Anderson, Chip. June 2003. "Higher Education Through the Lens of Strengths." Lecture. Azusa Pacific University, Azusa, California.

Bellah, Robert N., Richard Madsen, William M. Sullivan, Ann Swidler, and Steven M. Tipton. 1985. *Habits of the Heart*. New York: Harper and Row.

Buechner, Frederick. 1982. *The Sacred Journey*. San Francisco: HarperCollins.

Cloud, Henry. 2013. *Boundaries for Leaders: Results, Relationships, and Being Ridiculously in Charge*. New York: HarperCollins.

Csikszentmihalyi, Mihaly. 1996. *Creativity: Flow and the Psychology of Discovery and Invention*. New York: HarperCollins.

Csikszentmihalyi, Mihaly. 2000. The Contribution of Flow to Positive Psychology. In Jane Gillham (ed.), *The Science of Optimism and Hope: Essays in Honor of Martin Seligman*. Philadelphia: Templeton Foundation Press.

Csikszentmihalyi, Mihaly. 2003. *Good Business: Leadership, Flow, and the Making of Meaning*. New York: The Penguin Group.

Merton, Thomas. 1961. *New Seeds of Contemplation*. New York: New Directions.

Nouwen, Henri. 1997. *Bread for the Journey: A Daybook of Wisdom and Faith*. New York: HarperCollins.

O'Donohue, John. 1997. *The Invisible World*. Audiobook. Louisville, CO: Sounds True.

Palmer, Parker J. 2000. *Let Your Life Speak: Listening for the Voice of Vocation*. San Francisco: Jossey-Bass.

Pascal, Blaise. *Thoughts*. W. F. Trotter, trans., 1910. Retrieved from http://www.bartleby.com/48/1/2.html.

Plato. *Phaedrus*. H. Yunis, trans., 2009. Cambridge, England: Cambridge University Press.

Pratt, Michael, and Blake Ashforth. 2003. *Fostering Meaningfulness in Working and at Work*. In Kim Cameron, Jane Dutton, and Robert Quinn (eds.), *Positive Organizational Scholarship* (pp. 309-27). San Francisco: Berrett-Koehler.

Robinson, Ken. 2006. *Do Schools Kill Creativity?* TED Talk. Retrieved from https://www.ted.com/talks/ken_robinson_says_schools_kill_creativity.

Robinson, Ken. 2009. *The Element: How Finding Your Passion Changes Everything*. New York: Penguin.

Rumi. "Two Kinds of Intelligence." Poem retrieved from http://rumi-poem.blogspot.com/2013/02/two-kinds-of-intelligence.html.

Schaufeli, Wilmar, and Dirk Enzmann. 1998. *The Burnout Companion to Study and Practice: A Critical Analysis*. London: Taylor & Francis Ltd.

Twilight Zone: The Movie. 1983. Movie. "Kick the Can" segment directed by Lamont Johnson. Burbank, CA: Warner Brothers.

The Neverending Story. 1984. Movie. Directed by Wolfgang Petersen. Munich, Germany: Bavaria Studios.

Dead Poet's Society. Movie. Directed by Peter Weir. Burbank, CA: Touchstone Pictures and Silver Screen Partners IV, 1989.

Thoreau, Henry David. (1854; published in 2014 collection). *Walden and on the Duty of Civil Disobedience*. New York: HarperCollins.

Ulrich, David. 2002. *The Widening Stream: The Seven Stages of Creativity*. Hillsboro, OR: Beyond Words Publishing.

Whyte, David. 1997. *The House of Belonging*. Langley, Washington: Many Rivers Press.

Whyte, David. 2008. *Clear Mind, Wild Heart: Finding Courage and Clarity through Poetry*. Audiobook. Louisville, CO: Sounds True.

Wrzesniewski, Amy, Clark McCauley, Paul Rozin, and Barry Schwartz. 1997. Jobs, Careers, and Callings: People's Relations to Their Work. *Journal of Research in Personality*, vol. 31, 21-33.

Yaconelli, Michael. 1998. *Dangerous Wonder*. Grand Rapids: Zondervan.

Made in the USA
Monee, IL
07 July 2021